MW01065444

PIECES OF ME

PIECES OF ME

MY JOURNEY FROM AN
ABUSIVE CHILDHOOD TO A
LIFE OF HOPE AND HEALING

ROSE MARIE ABRAMS

AURORA PRESS

Copyright © 2018 Rose Marie Abrams

All rights reserved.

No part of this book may be reproduced, or stored in a
retrieval system, or transmitted in any form or by any means,
electronic, mechanical, photocopying, recording, or otherwise,
without express written permission of the publisher.

Published by Aurora Press, New York
www.mynameisrose.com

Edited and Designed by Girl Friday Productions
www.girlfridayproductions.com

Editorial: Lindsey Alexander, Michelle Hope Anderson
Interior Design: Paul Barrett
Cover Design: Rachel Marek

ISBN (Paperback): 978-1-7324963-0-9
e-ISBN: 978-1-7324963-1-6

First Edition

Printed in the United States of America

PREFACE

Two roads diverged in a yellow wood . . . I took
the one less traveled.
—Robert Frost, "The Road Not Taken"

I stand here at the crossroads of life, a middle-aged
woman, alone for the first time in my life. Who am I,
and what has brought me to this place? Looking down
the path to the choices that I have before me, I can't
help but wonder what or who has led me here? It is
true that I have taken the road less traveled, but why
did I make the choices I did? Is there any purpose to
everything I experienced, or was it all without rhyme
or reason?

What I do know is that this is not my first time here.
For those not familiar with the concept of reincarna-
tion, think of it like this: When the Creator designed
the human soul, He/She created it to be eternal. Since
the Almighty is unconditional Love and Light, we are

given more than one lifetime to learn and grow. It's something like the way a child starts in preschool and over time moves from grade to grade, eventually graduating from high school and advancing on to college and beyond. But unlike the school systems that many of us have gone through, we are not graded on our failures or labeled as being ADHD or learning disabled; instead we are given multiple lifetimes to work at our own pace as we evolve into higher spiritual levels of perfection. We ultimately stop incarnating when we reach the level of perfection that is right for us. In a sense, it is like the difference between someone who just seeks to graduate high school versus another individual who is not content with anything less than a postgraduate degree. Neither is right or wrong, they simply reflect the level of growth and learning the individual wishes to attain.

This is my story, or I should say our story, because I did not go on this journey alone. It is indeed a collaborative venture because, along with the helpers from the other side, in the form of angelic beings, there are others that contributed to this journey. Also, there were fragments of my original personality that developed as a result of the extreme abuse I suffered while living on what came to be known as The Farm. Though these fragments were technically still me, they came to the forefront of my consciousness and took over during times of severe abuse in order to secure my survival. Neither I nor anyone around me knew of this transition, as it happened seamlessly and quietly. It was only after I was in my forties and began reading the journals I had been keeping since 1994 that

I realized there was more than one voice being heard, voices that were very different from my own, and yet strangely familiar.

So what you are holding in your hands is not only my story, told in my own voice, but that of some of the other fragments as their words appeared within the pages of the journals that I have kept for twenty-five-plus years. I have chosen to honor them by integrating their stories into mine, permitting them to tell what happened in their own words and perspectives.

I have changed some of the names in this book to protect the privacy of those individuals who are still living.

CHAPTER 1

THE MAJOR PLAYERS

The opposite of trust is insecurity, and that has been the story of my life. Long before my birth, going back to the time when my birth mother was a child, the foundation that should have marked my earliest moments was shattered. The time was the late 1930s, after the Depression and before World War II. The place was rural Putnam County, New York, in the small town of Brewster. At the time, the village of Brewster was known as the hub of the Hudson Valley because of its iconic train station linking New York City with Poughkeepsie to the north and Danbury, Connecticut, to the east. It was also the home to the Borden milk factory, which produced Eagle Brand Condensed Milk during the late 1800s. The factory closed in the early

1900s when the local farmland was flooded to create the Croton Reservoir system.

By the time my mother, Viola Francis Williams, was born in 1937, the large hundred-plus-acre dairy farms had diminished, but there were still several in operation, though on a smaller scale. Viola was born to George and Jennie Williams, the youngest of eight children, on July 2, 1937, in a small cabin in Lake Carmel, New York. George, a decorated World War I veteran, was gassed on the battlefield and left for dead while serving with the First Machine Gun Battalion, First Division in France. Three days later, when the medical corps came to remove the corpses, it was discovered that George was still alive, though seriously wounded from a bomb that sent shrapnel into his upper body. The doctors removed as many of the fragments as they could. However, because of where some of the pieces lay in proximity to George's spine and lungs, they left some shrapnel in place. Upon his discharge from the army in 1919, and despite his disability, George married his high school sweetheart, Jennie Lounsbury, a petite dark-haired beauty, with hair that hung down below her waist. The following year their first child, George Jr., was born, and over the course of the next seventeen years, seven additional children followed, five girls and two more boys.

To support the growing family, George found work wherever he could, primarily as a migrant farm worker on the various farms in Putnam, Westchester, Rockland, and Orange Counties in New York, and also in northern New Jersey. The days were long and the work difficult. During the winter months, George cut peat moss out of the bogs and marshes to sell to customers to heat their fireplaces. George was in constant pain from the shrapnel that had been left behind in his shoulders, limiting his lung capacity and causing him to become hunchbacked. (He shrank from five foot seven to five foot two by the time he died.) But he never complained, thankful to have a job.

In December 1939, the unthinkable happened: Jennie was diagnosed with uterine cancer. The family was devastated. After a hysterectomy, she was sent home to recover. By this time, the family had settled down in Brewster, with George continuing to work the local farms during the growing season and doing odd jobs during the winter. By the following spring, it was apparent that the cancer had spread and Jennie was dying. The older children were capable of being on their own, and the eldest two, George Jr. and Hester, were already out of the house. The five younger ones, however, still needed supervision. Jennie suggested that they ask the county to take the younger children, because she knew that George could not physically care for them by himself. It was with a heavy heart that George agreed to turn the children over to the county. On December 6, 1940, Jennie Lounsbury Williams passed away. She was thirty-six years old.

In July 1940, Viola and her next-oldest sister, Bertha, nicknamed Bert, were placed in the home of a local dairy farmer and his wife, Mr. and Mrs. Salmon, who could not have children of their own. There had been rumors that Mrs. Salmon had been raped by her father and gotten pregnant by him, and that she had attempted a self-induced abortion; the resulting peritonitis had left her infertile, or so the story went. She desperately wanted a child, specifically a girl, to exact revenge for what her father had done, and these two young girls were among the first of the fifty to sixty foster children sent to The Farm, as it came to be known. Formerly the hundred-plus-acre Merrick farm, which had been in Mrs. Salmon's family since the early 1800s, The Farm at one time was home to chickens, rabbits, prized Holstein cattle, and draft horses to work the large garden and hayfields. By the time Viola and Bert arrived, The Farm was but a shadow of its former self, but it still had a small flock of chickens, a couple of rabbits, and pigeons. The white farmhouse had large, evenly spaced windows that faced east, allowing the morning sun to shine into the spacious interior. It seemed to welcome all who walked up the wide steps of the front porch, but behind the large oaken front door lay a dark secret. Instead of being a place of safety and security for the blue-eyed sisters with curly blond hair, it was a hor-ror movie with no intermission. The only reason that Mr. and Mrs. Salmon agreed to take the girls was for the monthly stipend the county gave them for expenses. Mrs. Salmon had deadpan, lifeless eyes that radiated no warmth, set into a sharply chiseled face. With her thin, pale, and lackluster straight hair that looked like it belonged on a scarecrow, she would have been a com-ical sight except for the fact that Mrs. Salmon—or, as she came to be known, Mother—was a very dark soul. She made no bones about how she hated children and saw to it that they were nothing more than slaves she could use to run the farm and the house.

When Viola turned five and Bert was nine, the family dynamic changed considerably with the addition of a four-year-old brown-haired green-eyed boy who looked like he had seen too many things already in his young life. Harold was his name, and his story was very different from Viola's and Bert's. Unlike the girls' mother, who had died, Harold's birth mother was only twelve years of age. She had been raped by a traveling glass salesman, and when Harold was born, he'd been placed in the foster care system until a suitable couple could be found to adopt him. Harold stayed with one family for the first four years of his life and then was placed with the Salmons. A few weeks after his placement with them, the couple received a call from Social Services asking if they wanted to formally adopt Harold as their own. Although Mother did not want to, she reluctantly agreed, seeing how happy Mr. Salmon was to have the boy in the home. The adoption proceedings were carried out in the summer of 1942, and Harold's name was changed to David. Now Mother had what she had always wanted, a child of her own.

Over time it became apparent that David was treated differently than the foster children, who now numbered six, with Bert and Viola being the youngest. To Mother, David could do no wrong because he carried the Salmon name, while the foster children, whom she always had thought of as second-class citizens, were now treated as if they were little more than farm animals. After David's adoption, Mother turned angry and physically violent toward the foster children, especially Viola, the youngest. Why Viola was selected, no one knows for sure, but it was the little five-year-old who was forced to do the housework before going to school and then to help in the garden and with the farm chores after school. Slacking off or not finishing her chores invited serious punishment and torture of all kinds, including being beaten, kicked, slapped, and punched, and having her head slammed against a concrete wall. Through it all, Mr. Salmon, whom the foster children called Daddy, seemed unaware of what was happening to the children. Daddy left the disciplining of the children to Mother, since she had the most experience with children. He worked long hours on the farm, and also as a landscaper on neighboring properties. He was of average height with thinning brown hair and brilliant, deep-set blue eyes. He was a man of few words, and never seemed to show many emotions. He rarely smiled or laughed, but when he did, his eyes lit up and his deep, gravelly voice rumbled like a freight train.

Mother had gone to college and had been a teacher at the local one-room schoolhouse prior to their marriage. He felt that she knew what was best when it came to raising children. When the foster children started coming to the dinner table with bruises and welts, especially Viola, he chose to believe what Mother told him, that they had fallen and injured themselves while playing in the yard or at school. The children said nothing of the truth, for fear that more physical punishment would follow when Daddy was out of earshot. It was becoming apparent to all who lived there that Mother ruled the house, and everyone knew to keep quiet about what was happening, especially when the caseworkers from Social Services came each month to do a well-child check.

Fifteen years passed, and the abuse continued for Viola and the other foster children who lived at The Farm. The lucky ones were those who stayed only a few days at The Farm before either going back to their families or being adopted into another family. The unfortunate ones, like Viola, stayed until they were twenty-one. Since Viola was held back in school on two separate occasions, she did not graduate from high school until she was twenty. However, through it all, Viola maintained a fighting spirit, which helped her to survive. She graduated from high school, began work as a hairdresser, and a year later went to work as a nurse's aide. While still living at The Farm, she commuted by train thirty minutes south to the town of Mount Kisco, in northern Westchester County. Here is what happened next and how I came to be, as told in her own words.

I got a job working the day shift. If they needed someone for the evening shift or the graveyard shift, I was asked to fill in. I stayed on the day shift for approximately two weeks, and then I went on the evening shift for about a month. I transferred to the evening shift, which I liked very much. It was not that hard. My main job was to take temperatures, check blood pressures, and prepare the patients for their dinners. I also gave back rubs and settled them down for the night.

One night, as I was running late, I knew that I wouldn't make the train on time. I called for a cab. It only took a few minutes from where I worked to get to the train station. The cab driver said he wouldn't charge me on one condition, that I would go out with him one night the following week. He also told me his name was Daniel, and I told him mine. I was off the next two days, so I didn't see him again until the following Monday. Checking the schedule at work, I saw that I was to work the whole week until Thursday and Friday.

When I saw Daniel again, I told him when I was off. We agreed to go out on Friday. I didn't care what [Mother] thought. I found myself falling in love with him. Daniel was the first man in my life, and I figured that it had to be love. Friday was my birthday, and it was also one year since I had graduated from high school. When Friday came, I just told her a little about Daniel and that I was going out with him. I was surprised that the only thing that she said was the fact that she wanted to meet him. He pulled up in front of the house and came up to the front door. I introduced him to the family and then we left, but not before she told me not to stay out too long. Here I was, twenty-one, of legal age, and she was telling me when to come in. I knew that I would listen to her, as I was too scared of her. He took me to a nice restaurant, and then we went down to the lake. We kissed for a while, and he started to do things that I knew nothing about. He asked me if I had ever "made love" to anyone. I told him no, and I wasn't sure if I wanted to learn. All I knew about making love was that in some way or another a girl could get pregnant. When I told him this, he laughed and said that he had some kind of injury and couldn't father any children. I didn't question him about this, as I thought I had found someone to love me. I even came home at a decent hour. The next morning I got up singing and feeling real good about myself. I saw him quite a bit after that. He would take me home from the hospital when I got off duty. Everything went fine for a couple of weeks, but what I didn't know was that [Mother] had the other children checking up on him. When I found out about it, I became really annoyed, but I didn't say a word.

The beginning of August, I started waking up feeling sick. I thought I had a case of the flu, however, it continued into the next morning. At that time, I had gone back to the day shift. It seemed that things that never used to bother me now bothered me very much. I would get dizzy and very nauseous. I was off for the weekend, and I was in the kitchen peeling apples for a pie. When I was ready to make the crust, I excused myself to make a run for the bathroom, as I felt extremely nauseous. When I came back and started to roll the crust, I was not prepared for what took place next. My foster mother came right out and said I was pregnant. Suddenly, I felt very weak, but I didn't let on to her what I felt. She also said that Daniel was married. I tried to tell her he wasn't, but she wouldn't listen. At that point, I wanted to walk right out of the house and never return. However, I had no place to go and nowhere to get help.

As unusual as it sounds, the family doctor, a kindly older man by the name of Dr. Cleaver, always made arrangements to see The Family on a Friday night in early September for our annual cold shots. I don't know why he had us come then; it was just something that we did. After we all had our shots, she sent the other children out to the car, except me. I thought she [Mother] would go to the car, also, but she didn't. She just stood there watching the whole exam. The doctor confirmed what she already knew. He said I was at least five or six weeks pregnant. While I got dressed, the doctor and she had a conference. I don't know what it was all about; I was too happy to worry about it. I was going to have a baby.

My joy was short-lived, though. We went downtown to get ice cream cones. While the others went into the store to get the ice cream, she turned around to me and told me to get rid of "it." She said she knew of several places that would do it. I just looked at her and said that I was not a murderer and I wanted nothing to do with an abortion. I was going to bring this baby into the world. I knew that she was mad, but I didn't care. I also still kept my job at the hospital.

I was off the night that Daniel called. I didn't feel like going out with him. I told him what I had learned. At first, he didn't say anything, and then he said that he guessed the doctor must be wrong. To prove that he was not married and that he loved me, he said he was going to Canada over the weekend and that he wanted me to go with him. The next morning I left with a packed suitcase. Ellen, one of the foster children, tried to stop me, but I wasn't prepared to stay and I told Ellen so. I told Ellen that she had done enough damage, spying on me and Daniel and saying that he was married. I told her he wasn't and that I was going away with him.

I waited at the place he had picked out for more than an hour. Finally, I called the number he had given me. All my fears were confirmed when the person who answered the phone said he had left for Canada with his wife and daughter. I just stood there and cried. How could he have done this to me? He had given me a beautiful engagement ring to prove to me that he wasn't married.

I didn't know what to believe. The hospital where I worked had rooms for employees who wanted to stay there. I went into the office and told them that I wanted a room for a few days. They didn't even question me. They just gave me the key and told me where the room was. I was off that day, so I just thought I would rest the whole day and try to figure out what I was going to do. I was deeply in love with Daniel. I knew that I would never do anything to hurt a human being that was growing inside of me. It was close to five p.m. when I finally awoke, and I had to eat something, so I went to the hospital cafeteria. I kept the room for a couple of days, and then I decided to go back home. I made up my mind that I wasn't going to listen to [Mother] and her ultimatums about aborting this precious new life. I also quit my job at the hospital, though I didn't want to tell her about that. I realized I had to tell her sooner or later.

She and I were the only ones home the next day. It seemed that while I was gone, she had called and told my sister, Bertie, who was living in Pennsylvania with her husband, John, and their baby. The arrangements had been made for me to stay with her and her husband. This way, I could "help" with their eight-month-old baby, Penny. I was so excited that I could hardly wait for them to come and get me. I packed my suitcase with everything that I thought I would need.

We left a little after nine a.m. the following Saturday morning. I, up to this point, had not been out of New York State. This was a four-hour trip. I sat in the back seat with Penny, the baby. It was a fun trip, and there was not one word about me being pregnant. We stopped for lunch, but I don't remember where it was. Just when I thought we would never get to their house, we pulled into the driveway.

The outside of the house was very pretty, and I hoped that the inside looked the same. I didn't have to worry about that, because it did. A big kitchen stood just off the front door, and down a long hallway was the bathroom, and farther down were bedrooms on either side. We had a light snack, which I didn't want, but I was told that I was eating for two now and I had to try to eat something. Bert fed the baby and put her down for a nap. I told her I felt tired and I wanted to lie down . . . I must have slept.

However, the idyllic situation that Viola seemingly found herself in had a dark cloud hanging over it. It was no accident that Viola had been sent to live with her sister, Bert, who had lived at The Farm until she joined the army after high school. Though she also had been abused, Bert had learned how to keep their foster mother appeased, and now the cycle had come full circle. Unbeknownst to Viola, Bert was under Mother's orders to do whatever it took to force Viola to sign over the child she was carrying to Mother. Even with all of the foster children at The Farm, the vast majority of them girls, Mother still did not have a girl that belonged her. However, that was all about to change, because Viola was the perfect person to deliver that child to her, because she was pregnant and not married. Having spent five years in active military service, Bert knew how to take orders. It was her job to see to it that the child, if the baby was a girl, was given to Mother as soon as she was born. Bert was determined not to think about what had happened to her or her sister, nor about what the future might hold for this child in Mother's hands. Instead she set about convincing Viola that it was in her best interest to sign the paperwork terminating her parental rights before the birth, so there would be less of a chance that Viola would change her mind and try to keep the child.

From the beginning of her stay, Viola was subjected to Bert's daily "talk" about how it was in the best interest of the baby to see that it had a "good" home with the foster family. How The Family could provide a much better environment than Viola could because she was not married, and Mother and Daddy were more experienced at raising children. The more the topic came up, the angrier Viola became. After all, this was her child, not Mother's. It was the first thing that she had that was all hers. She was not going to turn the baby over to the very person who had made her life so unbearable. No, it was not going to happen. NO, she would never do it. NO. NO. NO. This baby was hers and hers alone. She would be the best mother she knew how to be. She would learn by practicing with her niece, Penny.

The daily verbal assault on Viola was compounded by letters from Mother, who was alerted by Bert that Viola was not going to give up the child without a fight. Even Bert's doctor, Dr. Summer, who was also taking care of Viola, started telling her that the best thing for the baby was to "find a good home for it" because she could not take care of it as a single mother. Bert and Dr. Summer made plans: if the child was a boy, the doctor was to find an adoptive family willing to take him; if it was a girl, she would be given to Mother to raise.

The more that the issue was forced, the more determined Viola became to keep her baby. However, the stress began to take its toll on her. The morning sickness, which had abated, came back with a vengeance and reached the point where she was barely able to keep any food down at all. This only provided more fuel for the argument that she give the child up because, by not eating, she was not taking proper care of it. The cycle continued, which led to Viola not gaining any weight and simply struggling to maintain her weight. By her eighth month of pregnancy, she looked like she was only in her third or fourth month, having gained only eleven pounds. (The average woman gains twenty-five pounds during pregnancy.) By this time, Bert was expecting her second child and in her fifth month looked more like she was due any day.

Viola entered her eighth month of pregnancy in a state of severe depression, battling emotional exhaustion. She had reached the end of her ability to cope with the near-daily letters from Mother demanding that Viola give the baby over to her, because "it" belonged to her. Sensing that Viola was teetering on the brink of a breakdown, Bert suggested that they have a girl's night out and go to a nearby school gym where an old-fashioned square dance was being held. To Bert's surprise, Viola agreed to go and seemed to enjoy herself as she do-si-doed, sashayed, and swung around the floor. As the night wore on, Viola started to have sharp shooting pains across her lower abdomen that radiated into her back. Viola asked Bert if it was possible she was in labor, and Bert told her no, because she wasn't due for another month. More than likely it was false labor, and a good night's sleep would make everything better.

With that bit of advice resounding in her mind, Viola went home to bed and tried to sleep. Instead of the pains subsiding, they continued to come in waves every ten to fifteen minutes. Midnight turned into one a.m., one a.m. turned into two a.m., and two a.m. into three a.m. At four a.m., a scream of pain and fear shattered the night air as Viola hysterically called for sister: "Bertie, come quick! Where are you? Oh, my God, something's wrong with the baby!" Bert ran to the bathroom and found Viola doubled over on the floor, lying in a puddle of amniotic fluid, and in active labor. This baby was not waiting for Easter to come but had instead chosen St. Patrick's Day for the grand entrance. Bert called the doctor, who told Bert to get the mother-to-be to the hospital as soon as possible.

When Viola arrived at the hospital, Dr. Summer confirmed that she was in active labor, but in his estimation, the baby would not be born until suppertime, and in the meantime he advised Viola to get some rest and Bert to go home and wait to hear from him. As for him, he was going to go get a cup of strong coffee and take a quick nap, as he had just delivered another baby an hour before. The time: five thirty a.m.

The nurses attending Viola soon realized that this baby was not going to wait until the dinner hour to be born, and they all moved into action. One yelled down the hall to the departing doctor to come back, while the others tried to wheel the now panic-stricken new mother, who was in the throes of trying to push the little life out, into the delivery room. Viola never made it there, as the baby was born right outside the delivery room doors. After the birth, the new mother was moved into the delivery room so the baby, a boy, could be cleaned up.

As the doctor waited for the delivery of the placenta so that he could go find a badly needed cup of coffee, he prepared the speech that he would give to the adoptive parents, congratulating them on the birth of their new son. Since Viola had been awake for the birth, the story she was to be told was simple: "I'm sorry to be the one to tell you this, but your child was stillborn and has been buried on the hospital grounds."

However, the good doctor was not prepared for what he saw next. Instead of delivering the placenta, there was another head crowning. Viola had been carrying twins, and no one knew it. This was certainly not going according to the plan that had been formulated during the previous months. The baby boy was already spoken for; what if this one was another boy? What then? He could not falsify the records to make it look like this one was also a stillbirth, and not wanting Viola to know that there was a second child on the way, Dr. Summer said to those around him, "Oh, my God, there's another one coming—quick, knock her out!" Until the late 1970s, it was not uncommon for women to be placed under anesthesia when giving birth. In fact, "knock her out" were the last words my mother remembered hearing before she woke up the maternity ward of the hospital.

At 5:50 a.m., a tiny waif was born with the cord wrapped around her neck twice. Releasing the cord and administering oxygen to the infant, the doctor soon saw that the baby was breathing on her own. The only thing left to do was to get the child to cry; however, no matter what he did, no sound would come. It was as if the baby didn't want anyone to know that she had arrived in this world. After what seemed like an eternity, the baby eventually let out a small squeak, and the doctor seemed content with that. That little waif was me. In a strange way, I already knew that the world was not a safe place, and the only way I could survive was to stay as quiet as possible.

Since this was not my first incarnation here, I wasn't sure if I wanted to stay with what my soul had charted for me to learn this time around. Part of me wanted to turn tail and run back through the birth canal, into the tunnel through which our souls enter and leave this plane of existence, and to the safety of the other side, also known as heaven. I knew what the atmosphere was like—dense and heavy and negative. I longed for the essence of light and love that the Creator infused the other side with; however, it was that essence that pushed me forward, into the unknown that is life on this planet. I am a fighter, I always have been, from eternity past, and I wasn't going to quit now. There are five places in the life chart we meticulously plan out before our incarnation, called exit points, whereby we can opt to go home if we feel that our job on earth is done. I said no to the first exit point.

My soul had planned out this incarnation ahead of time, before I came here, right down to the last detail, and I was not about to back out now. This planning is done prior to our physical birth, in conjunction with our spirit guides, those souls who have passed over and now act as helpers/counselors both prior to and during our incarnation here on earth. When someone says, "Something told me to do X, Y, or Z," that is usually their spirit guide relaying a message to them. It is also known as intuition or gut instinct. Along with our spirit guides, we also work with our guardian angels and other celestial beings known as the ascended masters on earth, such as Jesus, Buddha, and Moses. With this finely detailed chart in place, I knew that I had to stay for the time being, though I didn't want to. I knew that I was here to help this woman, Viola, whom I would call Mom, as well as learn how to not only survive but thrive.

The first time that Mom saw me at my birth weight of 5 pounds 13 ounces, she exclaimed, "You look like a drowned rat!" Sure, I was hairless, but still, was that what every new mother says to her baby? The first feelings of rejection rippled through my soul. As I was placed on her abdomen, I picked up my head and looked her right in the eyes. It was as if I was trying to see into her soul. I wanted to know if she was someone I could trust. Here I was being introduced to the woman who had given birth to me. However, this was not the happy reunion between a mother and the child she'd carried within her body and could now see and hold in her arms. The first face-to-face meeting marks the beginning of the bonding process, but for Mom and me, that was not the case. From the beginning, I was afraid of her. I sensed her rage at the circumstances that I had been born into through no fault of my own. I knew that at this time there was no real love between us; it was all superficial. When Mom tried to feed me, I turned my head away from the bottle she attempted to put into my mouth. I closed my eyes and went to sleep, as it seemed that was the only way I could get away from her. The more Mom tried to feed me, the less I responded to her overtures. All I wanted to do was sleep; eating was not a concern to me.

May I break in here? My name is Norman, and I am one of the fragments that developed over the years to act as a narrator and relate the story of what happened to Rose.

Specifically, it was my job to gather the information from the inner children that live in the world of Rose's psyche and put it all together into a cohesive tale. These inner children are also fragments of Rose's psyche that came into being when the woman Rose calls Mom seemingly abandoned Rose and the abuse began. Many of the children are preverbal, so they telepathically show me what it is they want to say, and I translate this into words. Concerning Mom and the first time she saw her newborn child, just hours after the birth, one of the children, Infant Rose, has stepped forward to tell her own story of her first impressions.

Infant Rose: The nurses don't care about me. They don't care that I hurt. No one cares how I feel about being taken out of my nice warm home and into this horrible place. [She is describing the process of being born.] The yellow-haired lady [Mom] does nothing to stop them. The yellow-haired lady is supposed to mean something to me; she is what they call a mother. She scares me. I don't know why. I don't feel safe with her. I think I will go to sleep. The darkness is inviting, it is so warm and safe. I don't have any pain here. I float along on a warm sea of gentle, shifting waves. Back and forth, back and forth, back and forth. This is all I want to do, just rock back and forth, but the rocking now is not as gentle. It becomes more violent. I'm going to fall. I'm going to drown. And what's this? Some foreign object is being forced into my mouth. I don't want it. It tastes funny. All I want is sleep. The strange yellow-haired lady is talking to me again. She is saying strange things, sounds that don't make any sense. Things like "eat," "food," "bottle," "love." She scares me. I feel something bad about her. I do not like her at all. All I want to do is go back to my cocoon where it was dark and warm. I hear another strange voice. I feel myself being passed to someone else. [Mom had a roommate who had miscarried her sixth child. When the roommate noticed that Mom was struggling with trying to feed me, she offered to see if she could get me to take the bottle.] This is not one of the nurses, dressed in white with their funny smells. This lady is nice. She talks gently to me. She sings to me. I look at her. I like her. I want to stay with her forever and always. Her touch is gentle; there is no hate here. She offers me that funny-tasting thing, but this time it's different. Good-tasting stuff comes out of that thing. It feels good and warm. I relax again. This lady with the graying hair and lined face makes me feel safe. As she coos to me, I feel heavy and my tummy feels full. Once again I feel the boat rock gently side to side. I relax even more. I am once again adrift on the warm, inviting sea.

Mom knew deep in her heart there was a strong possibility that Mother would find a way to take me away from her, so she refused to give me a name. To Mom's way of thinking, giving me a name meant that I belonged to her, and she had already had so much taken from her that she could not bear the thought of having me taken as well. For three days I was known as Baby Girl Williams. By denying me a name, it was easier for Mom to not bond with me. The nurses, however, would not let me go nameless and gently forced Mom into a corner, telling her that I had to have a name before they could release us from the hospital. Mom chose the first name that came into her head, Rose Marie, which means "beautiful fragrance."

By this time, I was used to the bottle, and I soon began eating everything in sight, downing eight ounces of formula at almost every feeding. (The average newborn usually takes in two to three ounces per feeding.) Like Garfield, the cartoon cat, all I did was eat and sleep. While the other babies would awaken and cry, the nurse had to wake me up every four hours to eat, and half the time I would sleep through the feeding, drifting off as if eating was not all that important.

After a six-day stay at the hospital, it was time to go back to Bert and John's house, and to a new life for me. While the hospital nursery had felt comfortable and safe, the environment at the house was less so, especially for a preemie such as myself. The air was thick with John's cigarette smoke, forcing my lungs to work twice as hard as they should have. I was susceptible to all the germs and viruses that were part and parcel of living with an active fifteen-month-old, my cousin, Penny. At the age of five weeks, I picked up what everyone thought was a simple cold, but it quickly turned into a case of double pneumonia, from being exposed not only to Penny's cold but also to cigarette smoke. This is where all the eating I had done really helped, because the extra weight aided me to fight off the infection, and so did Mom rubbing Vicks VapoRub all over me to help me breathe. She didn't know that it shouldn't be used on an infant, but she was desperate, and besides, it worked. Within a day, I was remarkably improved. This was my second exit point. Again, I chose to stay, though there would be times when I seriously questioned that decision in the days to come.

While Bert had stopped telling Mom that she had to give me up to the foster mother, and while the letters from Mother had ceased, that didn't mean that the foster mother had forgotten about Mom or me. As soon as Mom came back to Bert and John's, the demands from the foster mother came fast and furious. No matter how much Mom tried to show how capable she was of caring for me, it was never enough. Becoming increasingly fearful that Bert or John would take me away from her, Mom began to take me everywhere she went, even to bed. She wanted to be damn sure that no one took me away from her, even when she was asleep. Several times she awoke in a panic because I was not beside her in the bed; Bert had put me into the crib, a place I seldom ever saw.

As the months passed, life settled into a normal daily routine of childcare, and Bert gave birth to a second daughter, Sarah. Shortly after the birth, a surprise visitor came to the door in the form of Donna, the eldest foster child that had been taken in by The Family. Donna was a tall raven-haired beauty and was considered to be one of the favorites among the foster children and often did whatever Mother wanted and needed done to keep the other foster children in line. There was no love lost between Donna and Mom, so it didn't surprise Mom at all when Donna asked to speak to Bert and John in private. Mom naively thought that the three of them were just catching up on all the news from The Farm, not once suspecting that something more devious was being hatched. Mother had devised a deceptively simple plan to take me away from Mom once and for all: to bring Mom and me up to The Farm for a weekend visit so everyone could see the baby. It was Bert's job to convince Mom that it was a good idea, and Mom agreed, figuring that the foster mother would not do anything if others were around.

Early on that fateful Friday morning, Bert, John, Mom, Penny, Sarah, and I set out for The Farm, arriving late that night. By this time, The Family had moved away from the actual farm. What they called The Farm was not a farm at all, but a large Victorian house situated on an old dirt road near the east branch of the Croton Reservoir. With its wide porch and expansive front windows, it begged all to come in and feel welcome in the cozy kitchen or near the fireplace in the warm, wood-paneled living room. The next morning, Mom came down the stairs with me, expecting to see Bert and the rest of the family in the kitchen or dining area, but the foster mother was there all alone. Bert and John had left very early, and Mom had been tricked. Mom and I were trapped with no way to escape, as Mom had no car, no work, and no way of getting either of those things in the foreseeable future. We were at the mercy of the foster mother, who was merciless.

It was here that my introduction to the foster mother, whom I would know as Mother, began. From the first day, Mother took control of me. At first Mom was not allowed to hold or feed me, and over the next few months, she was forbidden to bathe, change, or dress me. The frilly little dresses that she had brought for me to wear were thrown out, and instead I was forced to wear the hand-me-downs that came from Mom's own toddler days. Eventually, I was no longer allowed to be in the same room with Mom for fear that I might bond with her. I was isolated from the rest of the family because Mother wanted me to recognize only her. She was to be the only Mommy in my world, and I was to bond by force with her alone.

In order to achieve this "bonding," Mother used sadistic ritual abuse from the first day I was at The Farm. Under the guise of giving me a bath, this person who insisted she was my mother would plunge me into ice-cold water. She would also pour water over my head, causing me to choke and gag. If Mom tried to intervene, then I was pushed under the water and held there as punishment.

No one was allowed to bond with me, as Mother made it known that I was hers, and hers alone. No one included Daddy, but that did not stop him from playing with me and showing interest in me. He seemed to be happy to have me in the house and would go right to my crib when he came home from work in the evening to spend time with me. As I grew, he also began to read to me despite Mother's insistence that I belonged to her. It was those early experiences I held on to through the years, as they were the only signs of love and approval I felt I had.

In spite of the time and attention Daddy gave me, no one came forward to protect me from Mother's rages, with one exception. The only creature in that house with the courage to shield me from Mother was the family dog, a large German shepherd named King, and even his attempts proved to be fatal in the end. King was a one-man dog. He had only one owner, and that was Daddy. From the beginning, King would sleep beneath my crib. It was as if he knew what was happening and took it upon himself to try to guard me. He would not allow anyone to come near me, especially

Mother. I don't know how long this went on for, but one day King disappeared from the house. He was later found—dead. Someone had shot him.

As bad as the physical and emotional abuse was, there was something else going on, meted out by Mother herself, which she saved for special times, otherwise known as changing time. She was bound and determined to see to it that I would never become a woman or enjoy the act of sexual intercourse if I lived to adulthood. From almost the first day I arrived at her home, it became her ritual to inflict physical pain in the genital region by inserting diaper pins and other objects into my vaginal and anal areas, in effect both raping and sodomizing me. She did this under the guise of cleaning me, but the results were still the same. That is right, Mother raped and sodomized me when I was a defenseless infant. She was very careful not to leave any marks behind so that no one would suspect a thing; after all, she had had years to perfect her craft with the other foster children. Since I was now "hers," she could do whatever she wanted to me, and no one could stop her. Social Services would not protect me, as they were only concerned with the foster children in the home. Anytime my birth mother did anything to upset Mother, Mother attacked me. One of the reasons she used the sadistic torture was to keep my mother in line and to show Mom that if she did not obey Mother, I would suffer consequences.

Norman: This is why the original personality went to sleep and stayed that way. She was threatened with death so many times that Cassandra and I, as the adult personalities, and the children—Rosalita, Rosa Maria, Mute, and Euria—had to come out. They were all born because of this. She was not totally deprived of food or shelter, but of emotional closeness, the bonding that ties a mother to a child. The foster father did what he could, but he could not undo the damage that had already been done. Rose was left alone in a crib for hours at a time, because everyone thought that a quiet baby was a content baby. Quiet—yes; content—no. Given up, shriveling away to nothing. Slowly dying—just what the witch [Mother] wanted. Extreme emotional abuse. The child named Euria is the one who holds the pain. She carries it all—the abandonment, the yelling, the screaming, the physical abuse. She was born when the first attack happened in infancy. The shaking, the smothering, the attempted drownings—she carries it all. She cannot speak, but she weeps buckets for all those children who hurt, for she hurts also—the tears are her voice.

Cassandra: I'd like to add something to what Norman said. You're damn right that bitch controlled everything. It was like she was the queen bee or something. Where do you want me to begin? After it was discovered that Viola was pregnant, that very night Mother punched her in the abdomen repeatedly to cause a "spontaneous" abortion. When that didn't work, she sent Viola to her sister to be brainwashed into giving up the child; she sent constant letters, telling her to give us (she called us "it") over to her so she could destroy us once and for all. The dropping us off at that fucking freak show they called a house. She ravaged an infant so she could never have sexual pleasure, because it was our damn fault that Viola got pregnant. All under the guise of a diaper change—and, oh yeah, safety pins.

Even with everything that was happening, Mom still refused to terminate her parental rights. I was still hers, and there was nothing that would make her break the vow she'd made in the hospital the day I was born. Mom formulated a simple plan: she would get a job, save her earnings, and take us both away from Mother. She found work quickly at a dry cleaner and was thrilled to have her own money at last; however, her joy was short-lived. Possibly suspecting Mom's plan, Mother demanded that Mom pay the cost of our room and board, and it was the exact amount that Mom was making. So each week, Mom handed over her paycheck for "rent," fearing that if she did not do so, something terrible would happen to me. Little did she know that terrible things were happening to me whether or not she paid the rent. While she was gone, I was being indoctrinated in the ways of Mother's household. Rigid timetables, forced feedings, and the lack of any kind of comfort or bonding were the order of the day for me. I had no substitute for Mom in her absence, no cuddly, no pacifier, no stuffed animal or blanket. My allegiance was to be focused on Mother, and no one and nothing else.

Norman: One of the smallest inner children born during this time wishes to share her story. The speaker—if you can call her that, seeing that she is only a year or so old—is Rosalita, or Little Rose.

Rosalita: Don't make me go in there. Bars, everywhere. Nowhere to go. Can't get out. Cold, so cold. Mommy, I want Mommy . . .

Rosalita holds the fear of abandonment and the terror of being alone for hours at a time in the playpen or crib, which for her was a cage. Seems innocent, doesn't it? But it's not. The playpen is an instrument of torture, keeping unwanted ones confined and isolated.

The real question concerning Viola, the person I called Mom, was this: Who was this woman? She wasn't there to mirror back to me a mother's love and acceptance of me as person in my own right. To the others in my world, it seemed as if I was more of a nuisance, making more work for them. In the end, the only thing I had become was Mother's crowning achievement. I was her prized possession. Nothing more than a damned object.

Cassandra: One final thought about this point in time. Rose learned at this age that you can't trust anyone or anything. After all, look at what happened to Mom, as Rose calls her. Okay, granted she was not that bad compared to the bitch [Mother], not by a long shot, but shit, why did Mom leave Rose with the personification of evil in the first place? Trust? That was just not happening. No one really gave a flying fuck about her; it was all about the hidden agenda everyone had.

CHAPTER 2

THE TODDLER YEARS

The first boundary a child owns is a verbal one, the word *no*. The first time it is used, the child is signaling to the world that he has his own thoughts and desires, separate from those of the primary caregiver(s). On the other hand, since the child is not capable of making life decisions for himself, it is important for the caregiver to maintain control over the child, while at the same time respecting the child's right to say no, as it is a boundary, even if it cannot be honored.

When I was two, The Family once again moved, this time to an eight-acre piece of property that had once been part of a dairy farm that Daddy's family had owned. The house was bordered on three sides by pastureland from the still-working farm, owned by Daddy's nephew. The front of the house faced the main road and a giant hill that was covered with hundreds of deciduous trees, creating a canopy of green during the spring and summer and a riot of oranges, reds, and yellows in the fall.

In my life at The Farm, boundaries were forbidden, especially the word *no*. To say no to Mother was to receive physical and verbal slaps and kicks to the shins and any other place that she could reach. By having my ability to say no taken away from me, I was being trained to allow anyone to do anything to me. I had no symbolic door in my life that I could close and feel safe behind. My sense of safety was ransacked over and over again. It was if I were a rag doll to be tossed around, made into whatever anyone chose.

Cassandra: On behalf of Toddler Rose, I want to say: "No, bitch! That first boundary has become mine." I scream it from the mountaintops. I scream it in your [Mother's] face. "NO! NO! NO! I won't, and you can't make me. What are you going to do about that, bitch? What? You can't touch me—I will not let you touch me. If you try, I will kill you. Get away from me—I stand up to you."

Another hallmark of toddlerhood is the proverbial temper tantrum, as the child discovers that he is not the master of all he sees. The world around him also has boundaries that cannot be crossed, and the result of feeling that is anger. Anger, though often maligned as a "bad" emotion, serves an important function. It protects the ego by signaling that someone or something is a potential threat to one's survival. In my case, however, anger was a dangerous emotion for me to have. To express anger was to invite verbal abuse and physical beatings, specifically meant to break not only my will but my spirit, and they worked very well. From this early age, when I was upset or if Mother had punished me for some reason, I would quietly go into my room, shut the door, and not come out for a couple of hours. What I did in my room I do not remember, but when I did come out, I acted as if nothing at all had been wrong. Ask any mother of a toddler, and they will tell you that this type of behavior is not normal for this age group. Being denied the ability to freely express my emotions, even the positive ones, and in age-appropriate ways, is how the inner children came to be born. Their souls became the essence of the emotions that were not seen by the outside world.

Cassandra: Anger is for Rose's protection? Ha! Anger never got her anything but further abuse from Mother. Mother (oh, how I hate that word) cornered the market on anger. She was the only one who could show any kind of anger. No one was allowed to have boundaries at all. Having them would not do any good anyway because she would just blow them up with her withering words and physical assaults. After all, she was God, at least in her own mind.

When one thinks of mealtimes and toddlers, one may imagine a battle between well-meaning parents who want to feed their child nutritious food and the child who is just as determined to not eat what is in front of them. Once again, the child is attempting to assert his independence by controlling what and how much he puts into his mouth.

Norman: Speaking for the children who were there at the time, mealtimes were a crapshoot at best and a horror show at worst. The dinner table was where Mother dished out her most venomous tirades to the foster children right along with the mashed potatoes, so much so that Little Rose became very fearful of mealtimes. She could not wait to be excused from the table, but she had to stay until Mother was finished. It was prolonged agony.

Rosa Maria: Go away. She is there. She is looking at me. I want my Mommy! Where is Mommy? She is looking at me with this funny-looking thing. I see bars and eyes behind the bars [the tines of a fork]. Help me somebody. Somebody help me.

These are my early memories of mealtime at The Farm. These are not photographic memories, but rather my body remembering the terror of what it was like. Mother put me on a strict feeding schedule from day one, controlling not only mealtimes but how much I was to eat at every feeding. She also found ways to punish me for any number of things, most often by making me gag and choke on the scalding-hot milk she forced into my mouth before I was ready to begin to suck on the bottle it was in. She would slap my face and then force the bottle in again. My mouth was too small for the large nipple she used, and the opening gushed milk out of it and onto my face and clothing.

When I was nine months old, Mother took away the bottle, forcing me to drink from a cup. What little pleasure and self-soothing or gratification I might have gotten from the bottle was now gone. I was not permitted to suck my thumb; every attempt to do so was met by having it pulled out of my mouth and my hand slapped away.

More often than not, I ended up choking and getting whatever was in the cup down the front of my outfit. Mother saw this not for what it was, me trying to master a new skill that I was not yet physically capable of learning, but me rebelling against her, for which I needed to be severely punished. As she saw it, I was not drinking from a cup like a "civilized human being."

Having the bottle taken away also meant that I was forced to eat solid food—that is, whatever meal she had prepared for the rest of The Family; I was not given jarred baby food. As with learning to drink from a cup, I was expected to know how to eat solid food without being taught. Memories are now coming to the surface of having a too-large spoon forced into my mouth, filled with foul-tasting concoctions that I could not swallow without gagging. If you have ever fed a baby solid food for the first time, you know that it takes the baby some time to figure out how to coordinate the tongue and mouth so that the food does not come right back out again. When I pushed the food out in my attempt to learn how to swallow, it was seen as me "playing with my food" and not being grateful enough for being allowed to eat in the first place. Instead of being a pleasant experience, spending time around the table with family enjoying one another's company, meals were just another opportunity for Mother to wield her totalitarian control through verbal and physical abuse. Daddy was there, but I don't remember him saying or doing anything to stop her.

As time went on and I began cutting my first teeth, bigger pieces of food were introduced into my diet, including Mother's favorite: hard-boiled eggs. My first memory of being given hard-boiled eggs has stuck with me to this day: After putting a piece of the white in my mouth, I spit it out as I didn't like the slippery consistency and vile taste. Mother forced it back into my mouth, and I spit it back out. Screaming at me that I had to eat it, she then forced it in again and held my mouth shut, so I was forced to swallow it almost whole. The result was that I gagged and vomited it back up. Of course, that led to more screaming and yelling at me, with some slaps added in for "being naughty." This happened every time eggs were forced on me. I now realize that I was highly allergic to them.

Unknown Speaker: Gagging, choking, coughing, being force-fed some slippery, disgusting food. Throwing up, being slapped and told I was naughty. Being force-fed again. Struggling to keep it from going in, more gagging, more choking, cannot breathe . . . Bottle gone, forced to drink from big round object, water in nose, cannot breathe, choking. Metal object [possibly the back of a spoon] holding mouth open . . . strapped in high chair. Tied down, cannot move. Want out . . . cannot get away. Loud noises, loud noises . . . fighting. Make them stop.

By this time, Mom was no longer in the picture, seeing as feeding me was one of the first things that she was forbidden from doing when Mother assumed control of me. To ensure that no one else could feed me, and so that I recognized her alone as the giver of all life, I was forced to sit next to Mother. This way she could make sure that I ate everything on my plate and also brand me as her possession. She wanted me to know that she held my life in her hands, literally. To this day, I cannot help but ask: With all of this turmoil going on, how did I manage to eat anything? The answer is that I ate to survive, and nothing else. Food was not something to be experienced or, in a child's case, played with, as a means of discovering the world around me. It was meant to be choked down to keep Mother from becoming enraged and taking it out on me and the others who happened to be in the room. Since I was forced to sit right next to her, I was usually the one who had to take on her mealtime abuse.

Ultimately, the goal of this stage of development is to lay the foundation for self-identity, and the three most important words in that pursuit are *me, myself,* and *mine.* As with the word *no,* these words were also forbidden for me to use to describe myself or the world around me. In Mother's mind, I did not exist as myself but as an extension of her. There was no "me." I was a nobody and had to remain so. There were to be no first attempts at learning who I was and how I could do things for myself. Mother had decreed that I would never be independent of her, ever. The lesson here was not to learn how to do things for myself, but to learn how to be a miniature version of Mother.

A toddler's most important job is to learn what is theirs and what is not through the acquisition of boundaries. (This is not a one-time lesson but is learned over and over throughout childhood and even into adulthood.) For me, even the most basic boundaries were not tolerated. Boundaries separate the child from the parent, establishing each as an individual. Without boundaries, there can be no separation between the parent/caregiver and the child.

Cassandra: Look at the words: my blanket *(blankie) and* my teddy. *They are mine. NO ONE can take them away from me. NO ONE will take them away from me. Not now, not ever. You f**king bitch, how dare you take away my safety. It was mine, all mine.*

The flip side to the drive for independence is the development of shame. Shame is a boundary that shows us that we cannot always do what we want, when we want, and how we want to. It is the feeling that comes to the surface when we have done something wrong that hurts someone else, or violates our own moral code of ethics. In healthy doses, it reminds us that we are human and not God. However, when shame is used to keep the growing toddler from becoming independent, then it becomes toxic, leading the child to see himself, rather than his behavior, as "bad." At this stage the child cannot differentiate between who he is as an individual and his behavior. They are one and the same.

This is what I was born into, toxic shame. It was not what I did or didn't do, it was who I was.

Ms. Shame: I was conceived and came into being during this developmental stage. Shame describes who I am. I have eaten, slept, lived with, and breathed shame all of my life. I was born into a bad place; I was born bad. I need to be punished for being bad. That was Mother's promise to me. I was born to be punished. I was her bad self that needed to be punished, and I have taken on her persona in myself. I have become her persona in myself. I have become her bad self. I now do to myself what she did to me for years.

I was shamed not only for what I did or didn't do, but also for having the most basic of needs and for showing any emotion or feelings at all. If I did cry, which was not very often, I was severely punished for it.

Mother had several other methods of punishment that she used on me. Beginning when I was around twelve months of age, her preferred method of torture was dropping hot candle wax on my arms and legs. Other methods she used to keep me objectified were random slaps, pinches, and kicks, and sticking me with a diaper pin at changing time. These were used to scare me into silence, and they worked because I did not cry or even try to speak until I was almost three. When I finally started to talk, Mother would scream at me that I was a liar, and that I ought to be ashamed for not being able to tell the truth. No matter what I said, she said it was a lie.

In the end, shame defined me. I ate, slept, lived, and breathed shame throughout my toddler years, with Mother screaming in my face, "You ought to be ashamed of yourself" for every infraction of a rule that I didn't even know existed. She never let me live down the fact that I had been conceived and born out of wedlock, and was therefore bad inside and out and deserved nothing but punishment. I believe this is when my personality started to fracture and form individual parts that took on lives of their own. Over the years, I came to recognize them as "friends." However, over-shadowing all of my friends was the layer of shame, because they were shamed for doing what they were best at. It didn't matter what it was. These friends are one of the many gifts I now treasure. My "friends" learned early on to be silent, to go away and hide.

Unknown Speaker: I am Viola Williams's daughter. That in and of itself is nothing I should carry shame for. That is ludicrous—to carry shame for what my mother did? So what? What do her actions have to do with me? Nothing. I will not carry the shame for what another did. What other shameful accusations do you want to level at me? That I'm a whore, you say? From birth, you say? Guess what? I will not take that shame, either. A child is not a whore—that label is put on them by adults, sick, perverted people who cannot tolerate their own devious, perverted lifestyles. I don't accept that label any more than I accept that I am responsible for conceiving and birthing myself. Anything else? What's that? Shame for leaving her [Mother] alone? I am a bad person for being so ungrateful after all she did for me? Excuse me? Let me get this straight. I have to be eternally grateful for the sexual, physical, and mental abuse as well as the emotional garbage dumped on me? So what, I had a roof, clothes, and food. It would have been better if I were homeless or still with my real mother.

Norman: What you have read above is how the original child went away. She did not die, but she was put to sleep until it would be safe to come out again. Every time she cried, she was hit, because she was being "bad." That's how Arabella came about. Arabella holds all the rage of a two-year-old. If any of the inner children came out of hiding and were seen by the outside world (which was rare), whoever was out was hit, kicked, slapped, punched, and thrown, depending on the witch's [Mother's] mood of the moment.

Cassandra: Shame was Rose's first, last, and middle name. It's the second most popular phrase she liked to use for everyone from an infant to a senior citizen. We've been through this all before—so just for the lowlights: She was to feel eternal shame for being conceived and born. Yes, Sherlock, she willed Mom and the birth father to come together, have sex, and get Mom pregnant with her. That was the first salvo across her bow, and it's been going on ever since. She was to feel shame for just fucking being here, not being beyond perfect, and the big one, not taking her past and making it so that Daddy dearest (Mother's father) did not do what he did. Sure, no problem, one order of voodoo wipe coming right up. There, instant change—nice Daddy, beautiful daughter. God, I just want to vomit this right back up again. And, oh, by the way: not going to happen, bitch. Never going to happen. That shame that you dumped on me is coming back to you in spades. They don't even make enough playing decks to fill this order. What you do with your shame is your fucking business. This toxic waste dump of a life is closed to you, and your license to practice whatever it is you practice—and it sure ain't medicine—has been revoked. I, for one, am very, very glad that it has happened. Enjoy your stay in the Hilton Hell. Don't say hello to Satan for me.

I was also shamed for being sick; however, shame was not the only thing that was given to me when I was a toddler. As I look back at this time, memories come flooding back, some complete with pictures. Others are sensory memories, with no pictures, but with the feelings and reflexes still attached. One such memory is being sick with a cold, nothing major, just a stuffy nose, but that was enough to summon Mother for one of her favorite practices: torturing me under the guise of "care." For a cold, there were the alcohol-based drops that she forced into my nasal passages that made the inside of my nose burn as if it were on fire. The liquid would drip into the back of my throat, causing me to cough and gag while she held me down and slapped me.

Indeed no orifice was safe. Since Mother had to know everything about everyone, she kept tabs on everyone's bowel movements: size, color, consistency. If she thought that someone was constipated, out came the Fletcher's Castoria, a vegetable-based laxative—that is, for everyone but me. For me, she had another method of making sure that I was "regular": suppositories. In the memory I have, I was somewhere between the ages of two and five. Because she deemed I was being naughty and not going when I should, she made me lie on my side and then forced a suppository into my rectum. To this day, I still remember the gut-wrenching pain as it went in and her squeezing my buttocks shut to keep it in.

Another memory floats to the surface, begging to be recognized. As I look back, I'm more than just a little convinced that I had urinary tract infections, because I remember the genital pain and burning when I urinated, the not wanting it to hurt "down there," and being very aware of that area—too early, way too early. I couldn't say anything to Mother because she would yell, scream, and beat me. I suffered alone and in silence.

Physical and sexual abuse at the hands of this psychotic woman became a daily event. And as time went on, it was no longer just her, it was whoever wanted to have me. One was Mom's own brother-in-law, John, her sister Bert's husband. On Thanksgiving 1961, when I was just over two and a half years old, John molested me right in front of everyone. It wasn't until I was an adult that the full horror of that day came crashing through into my conscious memory. It was as if the years fell away and I was once again in that dark-paneled living room, sitting on my uncle's lap and feeling all the fear, shame, anger, and horror as he digitally penetrated me in full view of anyone who happened to be there. At the time, the house was full of relatives and foster children; some lived there and some had come back to visit. Most of the women were in the kitchen area, helping to make the meal and arranging the table and decorations, while the men were in the living room talking shop and sports. No one came to my rescue, because no one knew what he was doing. To them, he was just the friendly uncle getting to know the little niece he hadn't seen since she was a baby.

Later on, when I tried to tell Mother what had happened, with my limited vocabulary, I was met with words that I will never forget: "lying, filthy, white

trash tramp who willfully seduced a grown man."
Those words were accompanied by a severe beating.
She believed what she was saying, that a two-year-old
was capable of doing such a thing as prostituting herself, and what she said was always the truth. And then
there were the other foster children, who were now
adults and no longer living at the house, who acted
like drooling sycophants at her feet, eating up every
word—all too ready to turn on the weakest and tear
them apart for her pleasure. It was here that Mute was
conceived and birthed. I retreated into a shell in which
I became as silent as a tomb. I refused to speak, to cry,
to express any emotion at all. Stoic became my middle
name, even though I was only a toddler.

*Norman for Mute: Mute does not speak, yet she's the one that
holds the pain. She will tell you she was an elective mute, but
the truth is that silence was forced on her. Mute was born
long before that Thanksgiving, when the witch [Mother]
silenced her forever. "Liar," she called her, as she beat Mute
until there was no more to be said. Then she cut out her
voice box, symbolically speaking. Mute learned how to be
quiet and not say a word and to hold in all of her emotions,
good and bad. She has seen and heard so much, too much for
a little one. Mute will never be able to tell of the pain she has
seen or felt. She has been silenced forever, yet her silent tears
continue to fall, and will fall through all eternity. If you look
real hard, you can see her cowering in the corner, just like
a waif, a tiny little thing. Telepathically, she wants to say,
"Talk meant bad, very bad. Talk hurt. Me not talk. Talk bad."*

Because of Mother's rages and her vindictive ways of extorting submission, I disengaged my mind and acted without thinking. I wish I could say that I neither felt nor heard the cacophony of sound and the raining of blows upon my small body, but that would not be the truth. The truth is that, because of the severity of the torture, I split off, fracturing into many distinct personalities, each with a specific job that they did very well. Even at this young age, I was well aware that I was not the only one being physically abused in the home. The four foster children who lived in the home at the same time as me, all girls, were also subjected to the same physical, emotional, and mental abuse. On more than one occasion I saw Mother beating them, and I would run and hide in closet, for fear that I would be next. As time went on, I retreated to my fantasy world and someone one else would take over. Where I went during the time of abuse is unclear, but what is clear is that wherever the core personality went was a place populated by those who loved and cared for me. There were mothers and fathers who hugged me, who spoke quietly and gently. Their laughter was genuine, and they told me what a good little girl I was. They offered to play games with me and to read to me by the hour. They were very large and dressed all in white with long, flowing blond hair. They held me and comforted me in a way that no one had done before, and if it weren't for them, I would not be here at all. I have come to believe that these fantasy parents were not products of my toddler imagination but real Beings of Light or angels.

The episodes where I left my physical body stopped once I started to speak, around the age of three. However, by then I had learned to go into separate compartments in my mind. I had enough command of language to begin to put words to my imagination, and I would create all kinds of fantasies and stories. I retreated further and further into my fantasy world, which was filled with light and sunshine and warm summer breezes. Through this time, it was my vivid imagination that protected me from the verbal garbage being heaped on me. I trained my mind to go to those fantasy rooms when I saw Mother's rage and hatred toward my foster siblings reach a boiling point. This technique continued to serve me well. I would consciously leave, not physically, but in my mind. I would mentally check out into more enjoyable scenes.

Arabella: I am afraid of her ... She scares me ... She can hurt me ... She does not like me ... I want to be left alone ... No, I don't, I want my Mommy ... Where's Mommy? I can't cry because she [Mother] will hurt me. She is scary ... She is old and wrinkled. Why isn't Mommy coming back? I was mad at Mommy, and she went away, and I don't know where she went. I'm mad at bad lady, but she will not go away.

The Scared One: Go away—I'm very scared. The witch will get me and eat me. She will do bad things to me—because I am bad. She says I am hers, and she will not let me go.

Mute: If anyone sees me ... I will be hurt bad by the witch. She will yell, scream, and hit me because they noticed. I must hide—must run away before they see me. If I draw attention, then the Bad Witch will get me. I must be a wallflower. Cannot be seen or heard. No one can know that I exist—I am not here.

The Scared One: Feelings I cannot express. I wanted Mommy—the good Mommy, not the bad one. I wanted someone to make all the pain go away. Someone to pay attention to me. Fears, too many fears. No one to play with.

Rosalita: The large eye and hand; this is what I see. Go away, hand. You make Rosalita feel bad. Bad hand, bad, bad hand. Where's Mommy?

It is here, at the age of fifteen to twenty-four months, that I stopped developing emotionally and became a people pleaser. I stopped being an inquisitive toddler and instead tried to be good enough for a crumb of Mother's approval. Perhaps, if I was good enough, then I would be freed from being restrained in a two-by-two playpen devoid of any of the comforts a child needs—no blanket, no pacifier, no stuffed animals, no toys. Nothing to occupy my time or mind or hands.

However, according to Mother, since I was a bastard, I would never be good enough. I was something to be so ashamed of that I needed to be kept in solitary confinement. No one could ever know that I existed, the product of an illicit affair. This is how I spent my toddler years, isolated from the world, made to feel that I was something to be hidden away, carrying not only Mom's shame, but Mother's shame as well—the shame that she refused to acknowledge.

In the end, the question of "Who am I?" begs to be answered. Even though I look like an adult woman, developmentally, I feel more like an eighteen-month-old, caught in the internal conflict between independence and dependence. The most prominent emotions I feel are rage, grief, and depression, the emotions of a two-year-old who doesn't have the words to say how she feels. This is the child I am still trying to protect from the monster. This precious little one does not know that the monster cannot hurt her anymore. It's the two-year-old who looks out of the adult eyes. No one knows about the little ones that have been hidden away. They only show themselves in drawings and then only when forced to do so. I feel that I am only playing at being an adult. I am still a child in many ways, but I have covered it up with a veneer of adult responsibility. I was shamed for being a child back then, and all I feel is shame for having the same feelings now. I am supposed to be an adult, and yet I have never been a child, either. I feel the feelings of a child: fear, terror, and pain. There are more that I cannot describe, for they are beyond the vocabulary of a two-year-old. No one knows about the inner children except me. Will the inner children ever be safe?

Unknown Speaker: Mother allows me to live because she, in her omnipotence, has given me life. While it's true that she did not carry me in the womb for eight months, she thinks she has the power to decide whether I live or die, what I will or will not become. She thinks she controls me, but she does not—I am in a safe place deep within myself where she can never find me. I will never bow down to her.

Cassandra for Arabella: Arabella is having a meltdown. Arabella is the eternal toddler who wants her mommy, the comfort and security that only a mother can bring. She has severe separation anxiety and with good reason: her mother left and never came back. Arabella, the eternal two-year-old—angry and rageful at the world.

Rosa Maria: Why did she say she loved me and hurt me? Do pain mean love? Love bad. Love hurt. Bad lady go away.

Unknown Speaker: Everyone has left. Don't leave me. It's dark, so dark; there's no one here. I'm all alone. The sound is deafening. The silence—there is no sound. A wall of silence, silent criticism, silent blame, silent shame being hurled at me by those who stand in judgment of me because they would never do such a thing. Do what? I don't know. No one tells me what it is that I was supposed to have done wrong. I am bad, or so they say. Who are they? I don't know. Nameless, faceless people too afraid to show themselves, but their spotlights are aimed at me.

CHAPTER 3

THE ADOPTION

Three years after I was brought to The Farm, the final plan to take me from Mom was put into place, with the help of the foster children's caseworker, Miss Simpson. Miss Simpson was a tall, imposing figure with jet-black hair and a sharp, lined face that radiated a no-nonsense attitude. Her hawklike eyes saw everything, and when she did smile, which was rare, it never quite reached her eyes. During one of her monthly visit to The Farm to check on the foster children, Miss Simpson asked Mom to go to lunch with her. As if on cue, Mother offered to watch me so Mom could go, and despite her initial misgivings, Mom agreed to the luncheon date.

They went to a nearby diner, where Miss Simpson asked how Mom was doing, how her job at the dry cleaners was going, and if she had any plans for the future. Through all of the questioning, Mom became increasingly uncomfortable. Miss Simpson had never done this before, and Mom kept asking herself why the social worker was being so nice to her. It was rare for Miss Simpson to even notice Mom. Mom also noticed that Miss Simpson did not once ask about me, and that was when the red flags started going up. Pushing her unsettling thoughts aside, Mom tried to enjoy her tuna salad sandwich, but with little success.

Miss Simpson waited until after the waitress had cleared the table and brought coffee to drop the bombshell. The caseworker, on behalf of Mother, had decided that Mom should terminate her parental rights and give "the child" to Mother and Daddy to be adopted as their own. The reasoning was that, as a single mother going out to work every day, Mom had been neglecting the child by not taking care of her in the "proper manner." Miss Simpson continued by telling Mom that if she did not terminate her parental rights and sign the child over to Mother, then all the foster children remaining in the house would be removed and Mom would be held personally responsible for uprooting those poor children from the only home they had ever known and rendering them homeless. Even in the face of this threat, Mom firmly stated that under no circumstance would she give me over to Mother. She would take me and go back to Pennsylvania, where she had lived with her sister, and start over. Saving the best for last, Miss Simpson looked Mom right in the eyes and stated that if my mother attempted to leave with me, she would be arrested for felony child kidnapping, put in prison for the rest of her natural life, and have all parental rights terminated immediately. Miss Simpson went on to elaborate that Mom had been nothing more than a surrogate, carrying Mother's child for her, and now it was time for her to turn the child over to the "rightful" parent.

Mom began formulating a plan of her own. She would go back to the house and fill a suitcase with enough clothes for herself and me, confront Mother, leave with me, and never look back. But when she arrived home, I was gone. Only Daddy was there, and he told her that Mother and a relative had taken me on a weekend trip to upstate New York. Mom was told to pack her things and leave. She was being thrown out of the only home she had ever really had. It didn't matter where she went, as long as she was not at the house when Mother returned with me.

Being kidnapped by Mother is one of the few memories I have of this age, and even today, the emotions I felt during that time are just as real as when it happened. Terror ravaged my small body as Mother put me in the cargo bed of the relative's station wagon. Apparently, I didn't merit being put into the back seat but was relegated to the area where one would put the family pet. I didn't have a blanket or stuffed animal to comfort me, and for the first time in my three-year-old existence, I allowed my feelings to show. I sobbed uncontrollably, wanting Mom to come and comfort me, but there was no one. No one except Mother, who yelled at me to stop crying or she would spank me severely. I gradually stopped, more from exhaustion than from Mother's threats, and slipped into a restless sleep as the car traveled the eight hours to northern New York State and away from Mom.

Arabella: Why isn't Mommy coming back? I want Mommy now. Get away from me. You're not my mommy. I don't like you. You bad, bad. You old and you smell funny. I'm going to tell my mommy and she take me away, far away.

Arabella, my eternal two-year-old self, came into her own on the trip to northern New York. It was she who felt the roughness of the carpeting on the surface of the cargo bed. She knew how the barrettes felt when they bit into my scalp as I lay on the hard surface of the tire well without so much as a pillow to put my head on. It was she who screamed out her anger, rage, and terror at being ripped away from everything and everyone she knew, and for her troubles, she was threatened with further abuse.

One will never know for sure how this all went down. I learned about how my adoption came about from Mom many years later. Mom seemed to think that there might have been a conspiracy between Mother, Jean Simpson (the caseworker), and Mother's lawyer to get me away from her. At the luncheon, Miss Simpson had hinted that since Mom was not married, she could not raise me in the proper environment that Mother and Daddy could.

While I was being kidnapped and taken upstate, Mom was summoned to Mother's lawyer's office to sign the paperwork that would terminate her parental rights and give me to Mother. If she thought that she would find an ally in the family attorney, she was

wrong. She was told that based on the recommenda-
tion of the caseworker, it was "in the best interest of the
child" that she sign the paperwork. Just to make sure
that she understood completely what was being said,
the consequences for noncompliance were also spelled
out. If she did not sign the paperwork, she would go to
jail for life for noncustodial kidnapping. It was okay
that Mother had taken me because, according to the
lawyer, in the eyes of the law, Mother and Mom had
entered into a verbal agreement before I was born that
I was to be given to Mother and raised as her own.

Mom argued with the lawyer, saying that no such
agreement had ever been made, but to no avail. Mom
was given just thirty minutes to decide what to do.
The choices were simple: don't sign, and go to prison,
or sign the adoption petition and enter into an open
adoption agreement, whereby she would be able to
receive pictures of me and maintain extremely limited contact, as long as Mom did not tell me she was
my birth mother. My name would not be changed,
and I would be told the truth when I turned twenty-one. With a heavy heart, Mom signed. She was
given a date to appear in the nearby town of Carmel
at the Putnam County Courthouse for the adoption
proceeding to be carried out.

For Mom, that day came too soon, as it had only
been a couple of weeks since she had been told that
I was being taken away from her. Mom dressed me
in a lacy blue dress and combed my fine blond hair,
knowing that it was the last time she would be able
to do so. I cannot imagine the pain she went through
and could not show in front of me. Mother was right

there overseeing that nothing would go wrong with
her newest acquisition and obviously enjoying the hell
that Mom was going through.

At the courthouse, the adults went inside and I
was left to sit on a long brown bench just outside like I
was a piece of property and not a human being. Unlike
today, there was no child's advocate present to represent my best interests and to protect me from the
atrocity of what was about to take place. There might
have been a court officer there to watch me, but I have
no memories of anyone. All I remember is feeling ter-
ribly alone, again with nothing to comfort me and no
one to tell me that it was going to be all right.

Inside the courtroom, the judge asked Mom if
she was terminating her parental rights voluntarily.
Knowing the consequences for telling the truth, Mom
lied and said yes, she was. She could have blown the lid
off of the whole thing, but she was frightened and had
no fight left. She had no one to take her side, no lawyer to represent her. She felt she had no option but to
do what she did and pray for the day when she would
be able to tell me the truth. In the end, it was not the
physical beatings, the mental torture, or the sexual
abuse that Mother inflicted on her that caused her
to turn inward and retreat from the world. It was far
worse than that. The one thing that meant the most to
her, the one thing that kept her living and breathing
each day—me—was taken away from her.

Looking at the soon-to-be adoptive parents, the
judge said that the home background check proved that
they were indeed the "perfect" family to raise the child.
They were asked if there were any name changes, and

they replied, "Yes." My name was changed from Rose Marie to Margaret Rose. With that simple statement, I was transferred from the woman who had given birth to me to the adoptive family, as if I were an animal. My whole identity was wiped out, and a new one was put in its place. I was no longer Rose Marie (two words), but Margaret Rose (no nickname, shortening of the name, or pet name allowed), named after a long-deceased relative of my now adoptive father who had died in 1918 during the flu pandemic. Mom had been lied to, and Mother had claimed another victim. The adoption paper just solidified what had gone on from before my birth, only now it was public record and "legal." Mom's hopes and dreams were shattered.

Norman: Her role as the slave, the scullery maid . . . This was hammered home, and I do mean physically beaten home, every chance Mother got. The adoption wasn't enough. The name change wasn't enough. The strict orders to any and all in the household that she must never know who her mother was were not enough. It was literally driven home with sexual abuse and later mental torture combined with physical abuse.

Cassandra: There is a whole group of us that are as angry as hell. That our mother would turn her and us over to that bitch. She fucking knew what would happen and what was happening, and yet she still did it . . . We were forced to take that bitch's name and family tree. What's so great about that family? Don't know them from Adam, and don't care to. They were nothing to write home about—so what they were pedigreed? So's my Heinz 57 variety mutt, and it has more class, too.

This adoptive home definitely was not where my heart was. Nor was I told the stereotypical adoption story by gushing parents about how the newly acquired child was chosen to fulfill a years-long dream. Instead, I was the target for physical attacks not only by Mother but by my foster siblings. The foster children, some four to ten years older than myself, were insanely jealous of the fact that I had a forever home. I'd been adopted and now had a family, and they didn't. So to get back at me, a three-year-old, they would hit, pinch, trip, and slap me, and also pull my hair, knowing that if I cried, I would receive more of the same from Mother for interacting with them, which was against the rules.

The other foster children thought I was the "special one" because Mother touted my adoption in front of them, and they hated me for it. They never realized what I was going through. That I was actually one of them. I was just camouflaged to look like the enemy. They were only different because they had their own last names. They never knew how good they had it, because they still had a shred of their own identity. They could look at their parents and siblings and say, "I'm related to you, and I have a choice whether or not I want to have a relationship with you." I didn't have that. They never knew that the only social interaction I had during my preschool years was with them.

The isolation I endured sharply contrasted the rare times that company came to the house. One would not be blamed for thinking that I acted like a dog on those occasions; I was so excited that someone had come over just for me (or so I thought). I was hoping to be rescued because all I wanted was for someone to love me, to acknowledge that I existed, to tell me that they were Mommy.

I began to make bargains with Mother in my head. I told her I would do anything if she would be happy and not hurt me anymore. At the time, I didn't realize that she was ecstatic to be doing the one thing that gave her great joy: inflicting as much pain and torture as she could on those who were dependent on her. The more pain she could inflict, the happier she was, but there was one thing that stopped her from experiencing complete joy. No one could make enough sounds of pure torture—our cries and screams were never sufficient.

John was not the only person who violated me. Another foster child by the name of Ed, who was in his twenties and had grown up with Mom, did, too. Of average height, Ed had slicked-back black hair and eyes that showed no signs of life. Of everyone in The Family, he scared me the most. There was something about him my four-year-old self did not like, and I did my best to stay as far away from him as possible. One very vivid experience I have that will haunt me for the rest of my life happened when I was four. I had fallen asleep in my bedroom and awoke suddenly to find Ed standing by my bed with a camera in his hand. He was taking pictures of me as I slept and had snapped a picture of me as I startled awake. I had the photo for many years. The look of fear on my face is so prevalent.

There was more to that violation than just the picture-taking. He had molested me while I was sleeping.

The Scared One: I hurt . . . hurts down there . . . hurt any-where but down there. God, make it stop, please make it stop. Burning, stinging, sharp pain. I can't let her know.

Ed came around quite often because he worked as a handyman in the yard and kept a pigeon coop with a dozen or so pigeons on the property. I was terrified of the birds and being around the coop, and for years I did not understand why, but now I do. Especially during the summer months, Ed would take me down to the coop to "see the pigeons," and he would molest me. I have a vivid memory of one time, but I know that there were other times as well. This went on until I was seven.

I've never questioned whether Mother knew what Ed was doing to me, but rather how much she knew and if she told him to do it. If she did, what was the payment? Whatever the truth, my mind cannot begin to comprehend any woman condoning the molestation of a child, but then again, we're not talking about a normal woman here. I'm speaking of Mother, the epit-ome of evil.

— — —

Music was a means of escape for me. From the time I was very young, I could play songs on my little red toy piano. I would hear commercial jingles one time and then be able to re-create them by ear. It was more than just banging on the keys to make noise. There was something primal about hearing how the notes flowed together and made sounds that made sense. I could feel the energy of the notes. To everyone around me, it was just noise, but to me it was an escape into another world. However, Mother couldn't play, so she thwarted me from learning—as she did with every other potential talent—though that didn't stop me from playing whenever I could.

On rare occasions, Daddy would take me with him when he went to one particular customer, Miss Pierce, who owned a beautiful concert baby grand piano. Miss Pierce was a stately, elegant woman with a gentle face framing the most beautiful kind blue eyes that twinkled whenever she saw me. She could easily have graced an English castle with her statuesque frame and refined manners. She had never married, choosing to be one of the first female bankers on Wall Street during the 1920s, working in her father's financial institution. When I was a child, Miss Pierce lived in a large Victorian-style house perched on top of a hill overlooking fertile farm fields.

While Daddy worked on the grounds, Miss Pierce would invite me to play the piano. She had explained to Daddy that there was no one to play the beautiful instrument since her sister had died, and she wanted the sound of music to fill the house again. At the age of four or five, I pretended that I was a concert pianist, the baby grand piano was my instrument, Miss Pierce's solarium was my stage, and dear Miss Pierce was my audience. I would create musical pieces out of my imagination and just let my little fingers run all over the keyboard. She did not mind if it was too loud, as she really seemed to relish the fact that someone was enjoying playing the piano once again. More than once, Miss Pierce told Daddy that I had real talent and needed to have lessons. Daddy never told Miss Pierce that Mother had forbidden it.

Miss Pierce became the first person, an outsider, to give me the acceptance and approval I craved. I looked forward to the rare times I could go with Daddy to Miss Pierce's estate so I could play the piano. I loved the smell of lemon polish in the solarium and the curio cabinet filled with miniature antique mechanical banks that ate the coins when a button was pushed. Filled with sunshine, the solarium became my home away from home. I loved everything about the room, from its wide windows to the green plants everywhere to the baby grand piano that called to me from its corner by the door leading out to the garden. It was the exact opposite of The Farm, with its dark wood paneling and somber atmosphere. To be there at the old Victorian on the hill was the equivalent of finding an oasis in the desert, which helped me to survive the hell that was home.

CHAPTER 4

THE END OF ISOLATION

Kindergarten marked the beginning of my formal education, but more importantly, it also ended the absolute isolation of my first five years of life. However, this introduction to the "real world" was not easy or fun for me. I was absolutely terrified. I had never been in the outside world, except for the rare times I'd gone with Daddy to Miss Pierce's house. To someone like me, whose world had been confined to The Farm, the sights and smells of the large kindergarten rooms were overwhelming.

Back in the 1960s, in Brewster, New York, new housing developments such as Mountain Brook, Brewster Heights, Tonetta Lake, or Putnam Lake were being erected to house the large number of families moving out of New York City. For some of the children who lived in these developments, there were potential friends to be made and the opportunity to learn to socialize with other children their own age. I was not so lucky, as our nearest neighbor with children lived a quarter mile away, and in any case I was forbidden from playing with them because they might "contaminate" me with ideas that could turn me away from my forced allegiance to Mother. They may as well have lived on the far side of the moon. So for me, kindergarten was the first time I found myself with a group of children I did not know, in a classroom setting, and with a woman in a position of authority besides Mother.

With the beginning of school, I entered into what I have come to call "The Lost Years." I have very few memories of homelife and school during that time. What memories I do have, I would describe as being like fine Swiss cheese, more holes than substance. I do have several positive memories of kindergarten: Sitting in a circle at the front of the classroom listening to Mrs. Dallinger read to us. Sitting at my desk (it seemed so big at the time) and learning about the colors and what their names were. An especially happy memory for me was playing with the wooden jigsaw puzzles in the play area. I loved the smell of the linseed oil used on the puzzles and how the large wooden pieces fit into the outline of the picture so perfectly. However, what I loved the most was the fact that I could be by myself. Even at this tender age, I was a loner; whether or not they did it on purpose, the other children avoided me. Either they already had friends their neighborhood or the bus, or they'd already started making other friends at school. Eventually, I found myself on the outside of every group in the kindergarten class. I soon realized that I was different from my peers.

The reality is that I don't want to remember those times; it's just too painful. Beginning in first grade, I went from being ignored by my classmates to being openly bullied. I was the one that everyone picked on because I would not fight back. I just let them do and say anything to me, and never once responded to any of the taunts. On the playground, the other children dared me to climb up the fireman's ladder and slide down, knowing full well I couldn't do it. I was called a scaredy-cat, baby, and worse. I wanted the earth to open up and swallow me so that I couldn't hear what was being said. I knew that no one was going to come and rescue me. I began the slow retreat into myself, just as I had done at home.

School became just like home, a continuation of the emotional and mental abuse. There was no way that I could tell anyone at home what was going on on the bus, at lunch, or during recess. When the first-grade teacher, Mrs. Jerald, a fiery redhead, mentioned the bullying to Mother at a teacher-parent conference, Mother thought I was allowing myself to be bullied on purpose, to draw attention to myself, so she punished me for not staying hidden from view. It was my fault that I was having difficulty fitting in with the other students. Mother could not see that in fact I was her star pupil. No one wanted to have anything to do with me. I was different and I knew it.

Merlin: I came out when she first went to school, in the real world. No one suspected a thing. I was the one they saw, the quiet, shy little waif, but I couldn't help the little children personalities from slipping through occasionally. I can think of one time: once it was in kindergarten, finger painting in the art room. She started crying about putting finger paint on the paper, painting, I guess, a picture of The Family. One of the little ones did that; I don't know which one, but they were being reminded of something, though of what I don't know. Wouldn't you know it, the little one that started to speak disappeared; someone didn't want it revealed just yet, but you get the picture.

Art class was the one class we left the kindergarten classroom for. After going down the long hallway to the other end of the building, we entered the art room, which was relatively small and crowded with long desks and easels. I don't know if it was the time of the year—just before the Christmas holidays—or the fact that we had to leave the classroom that added to my fear and trepidation. This was to be an adventure for us five-year-olds, as this was our first time finger painting. The rest of the class was excited as we donned our art smocks, our dads' old shirts, and prepared to get our hands covered with paint. The objective was for us to paint a picture of what our house looked like all decked out for the Christmas holidays. For whatever reason, all I felt was blackness and absolute terror. The pot of red paint loomed larger and larger in my field of vision. Suddenly, it morphed into a giant container of red molten blood, and I was no longer in that small, cramped art room, but in a swirl of darkness with red streaks surrounding me. I heard Mother's voice threatening me with death, destruction. I sensed pain, unimaginable pain, if I touched the paint and told about the house. I knew what would happen if I got my hands dirty. I would be beaten. My fear and panic reached a fever pitch, and I became hysterical over red paint and the house. I can only imagine what I must have seen or heard or been subjected to that would trigger such a response.

After the flashback in the art room, things settled down for me. Slowly, I began to enjoy myself in the classroom, as we learned to write our names and learned about colors and shapes. However, that all began to change at the end of June when we had a class picnic at Southeast Town Park, next to the firehouse. While I don't remember much about the event itself, I do remember being afraid of the bathroom, which was little more than a concrete outhouse with open stalls. Either I was too afraid to go in there, or I couldn't make it in time, but ultimately I soiled myself. Mrs. Dallinger was very sweet about it. I cried hysterically, fearful of what Mother would do because I'd done a "baby" thing. While Mrs. Dallinger helped me clean myself off, word spread about what had happened, and as soon as I came out of the bathroom, the teasing and taunting began. I can still hear the other kids calling me "baby" and saying, "We're going to tell." By the time I was on the bus headed home for the day, it seemed that everyone had heard, and the teasing and taunting, this time from the older kids, began again. I became even more fearful of what Mother would do but didn't show any feelings because crying would ramp up the torture. I have no memory of what happened when I got home that night. I can almost guarantee it involved some form of physical punishment for garnering any kind of attention. Attention meant scrutiny by the teachers and school administrators, which meant Child Protective Services might get involved. The whole thing could blow wide open, and the rampant abuse of the foster children would no longer be a secret.

After this incident, I decided that I would not cry in front of people because I didn't want Mother, Daddy, or my foster siblings to make fun of me. It's all coming back. Even today, fifty-five-plus years later, I can still feel the raw waves of shame washing over me. Crying was seen not as a sign of weakness, but as a sign that I was less than human, only worthy of physical torture and abuse. Everyone bullied and tormented me, and I mean everyone, and I still remember crying for some long-forgotten reason, lost to the fog of history, and having Daddy tell me that it was time for the crying towel and bucket. I don't even know what that meant. All I knew was that only babies cried, therefore, I must be a baby. Never mind the fact that I had something to cry about.

The Child: I want to make friends, but I'm afraid that once they get to know me, they will see me like she sees me. She is the witch, you know. She is a bad lady, a bad person. She hurts everyone. She forbade me from ever having friends because they would take me away from her, just like she took the baby away from her mommy. I'm not the baby, I'm six years old, but I can be older, too.

First grade, where I first learned how to write and read and do math, brought its own challenges. I was a natural at reading, and it wasn't long before I was reading at an almost third-grade level. I couldn't get enough of books; they were my sanctuary, a place where I could hide from the rest of the world. However, it was not my reading skills that drew Mother's focus at this time. She could not have cared any less that I was in the top reading group in my class. Oh no, it was my "inability" to write legibly. First grade was when students began to learn how to write in block letters, and like any skill, it took a while to master. But Mother expected me to skip over block letters and do the more advanced cursive writing from the beginning. School nights became a nightmare for me, as she demanded to see all of my assignments so she could critique my writing, and it always ended up becoming a one-sided shouting match as she told me how sloppy I was, how illegible my handwriting was, and how I would never amount to anything. She called me all manner of degrading names and even took to mockingly throwing whatever I had written back at me. One time I mistakenly brought home someone else's in-class assignment, and she called me the other child's name before slapping me for not printing as neatly as they had.

As bad as the house was, the bus ride to school was even worse. Since I was the last stop on the bus run to school, there was never a place to sit, and no one would move over so I could sit next to them. More often than not, I was forced to stand in the aisle and hold on to the back of a seat so as not to fall. Even if the bus driver told kids to move, they wouldn't, and so I was often yelled at by the bus driver for standing, which only caused more teasing and bullying. As I write, memories are beginning to come back of being teased for having barrettes in my hair instead of having a ponytail or wearing my hair down. I was also teased because of the way my hair looked; it was cut very short, and the ends curled every which way. However, that taunting was small potatoes compared to the taunts thrown my way because of the incident at the kindergarten picnic, where I had soiled myself. Starting in September, on the first day of school from first grade to fourth grade, someone would say something about that incident, and the taunting would last until at least December.

I have almost no memories of second grade. I remember the teacher's name, but nothing else of the school year, except for one memory that continues to haunt me to this day, when the unthinkable happened: the school called Child Protective Services on my behalf. From what I have been able to piece together, a very courageous library aide, Mrs. Brown, saw something about me that raised her suspicions. What it was I can only guess, but she reported her suspicions to the school psychologist, who called Child Protective Services and my adoptive parents in for a meeting. A classmate told me many years later that two women from CPS came to the classroom and took me out and I was absent for several days. I have no memories of that happening, but I do know that after that point the sexual abuse stopped.

By the time I was eight years old, in third grade, Mother started to do everything she could to make me appear totally incompetent. She expected nothing less than perfection from me, and since I could not attain that level (indeed, not even God could), my feelings of being an idiot, an incompetent blob worthy of only her wrath, which knew no bounds, were formed and took on a life of their own.

With the advent of nightly homework assignments, Mother found a new form of torture. Homework was a means to show the world how incredibly stupid I was. Mother forced me to do every assignment "draft" style and submit it for her approval before writing the final copy, which she also scrutinized. This turned thirty minutes' worth of homework into a two-to-three-hour ritual complete with tirades about how careless and sloppy I was and how so-and-so (another child in the class) was so much neater, better, smarter, and more intelligent than I could ever be.

Tests and quizzes also merited scrutiny and derision. I had to do absolutely perfectly on them, and in order to make sure I did, she had to see every test and quiz grade, report card, and graded homework assignment. Even an A+ was not good enough for Mother. An A+ meant that the teacher was totally inept and could not see that my work was not beyond perfection. Only Mother's standards were good enough to judge me by.

It seemed that Mother's four years of teaching grades 1 through 8 in a one-room schoolhouse in the 1920s made her an expert in what was important in the 1960s classroom. In her opinion, the teachers were not good enough, especially the ones that encouraged me. For every encouraging thing my teachers said to me or wrote on my papers, she had ten bad things to say about my work, me, or even the teachers themselves. She knew what was best for me, and knowing I would never measure up to her standards just solidified in her mind the fact that the teachers knew nothing about what I could really do. Mother expected me to be perfect in every subject, from penmanship to math.

In third grade, the taunting and teasing by the other children intensified. Our class was selected to perform *The Wizard of Oz* for the school, and I was cast as the Wicked Witch of the West. Following the production, which went off without a hitch, the younger kids on the bus started calling me "witch" and other offensive names. This continued on the playground as well.

Fourth grade is another year I have few memories of. I do know that bullying, name-calling, and the rest continued, though it might have lessened just a bit, as I was now in one of the upper grades. I do remember we were supposed to select a musical instrument to learn how to play. For many students, this was a chance to learn an instrument they'd always wanted to play, or at least one that did not disturb their parents too much. As had been the case throughout my life, my choices did not matter; it was all about Mother, and she chose the flute for me because it was the quietest instrument and would not disturb Daddy. If she had her way, I would have not been exposed to any instrument; however, she had no choice. She permitted me to have an instrument, but with one giant stipulation: I had to know how to play it perfectly from the very beginning without having to take any lessons. Once I started taking lessons, I was forbidden from practicing because it would upset Daddy.

Fifth grade, my last year of elementary school and the beginning of my tween years, was also the beginning of womanhood for me. In December, as an early Christmas present, Mother Nature gifted me with a good case of the mumps and something else, my menarche. It was now official: I was becoming a woman. This development was not to Mother's liking at all. I'll never forget what she said: "I wasn't expecting it this early." Instead of the mother-daughter talk about the facts of life, she gave me a sanitary belt and a pile of cloth diapers and rags and showed me how to fold them and put them on. Except for the heaviest days, I was to use the diapers during my cycle instead of disposable pads, as the pads were too expensive to use on a daily basis. That meant wearing the diapers to school as well. I still remember praying like hell that I didn't have an accident while using the rags because I had no backup plan. I wasn't permitted to take extra pads with me, and in the event that I needed an extra, I had to go to the school nurse for one.

The physical sexual abuse had stopped when I was seven, but now the emotional and mental sexual abuse started. Every month Mother kept track of when my cycle began and how long it lasted. She also checked the rags to see how heavy the flow was. I still feel the humiliation and shame that would wash over me, as if being a woman was criminal. I was to tell no one that I was menstruating, not the girls at school, and certainly not Daddy or my adopted brother David, who was living with us at the time. It was as if I had contracted some sexually transmitted disease and had to be hidden away each month because someone might find out that it was "that time of the month."

Cassandra: She was Mother's little puppet on a string. She felt that Mother could read her thoughts—even they weren't private. Mother had to know exactly when her menstrual cycle was, or she would accuse her of being pregnant. Pregnant? She didn't even know what sex was. From the time she was an infant, Mother accused her of prostituting her body, and now her body was changing her into that of a woman. She felt dirty and shamed for being a woman. Mother controlled everything. How dare Mother control her cycle.

Despite it all, there were high points during my elementary school years as well. The outside approval and acceptance that had started with Miss Pierce continued into the first grade as my inner world began to interact more with the outside world. I was able to be myself more, and I began to blossom as I was praised for the effort I was putting forth in learning. However, at the end of each school day, I had to put away my inner world and return to being invisible as I got on the school bus to go back to The Farm.

Mother was deluded enough to believe that she could tell the teachers how to see and treat me. However, to my teachers' credit, beginning in the first grade and continuing all the way through to high school, they didn't share Mother's opinion that I was incapable of anything but the most remedial classes. The teachers commented in my report cards that they saw me as a quiet, mature, intelligent, and gifted student, with the potential to do great things. All I needed was the encouragement to try, and that is what those beautiful, gentle people tried to do. But no matter how much encouragement I received from the teachers, Mother was right there screaming louder than all of them put together. No one knew what she was doing because she always acted so nice at parent-teacher conferences. "Look at me, didn't I do such a wonderful job?" her behavior seemed to say. In her mind, all the hard work I was doing was so that she could look good; I was to never receive any credit whatsoever.

Cassandra: She was beaten, kicked, slapped, and God knows what else for talking, for being noisy and rambunctious; even outside she could not be a child, she always had to be quiet. The teachers all commented on how quiet she was. Some thought that there was a problem that she was so quiet, but they never knew the half of it. At home, she was being punished for being "too quiet" in school and for drawing attention to herself.

By the time I was in the fifth grade, I really enjoyed being in the classroom. Our teacher, Mr. Franklin, was progressive and brought a new style of teaching to our school, a style that was a good twenty years ahead of its time. He encouraged us to discover our own style of learning and to develop it to the best of our ability. He did not use letter grades, but rather descriptive phrases that defined our level of mastery of the subjects at hand.

For example, as part of language arts, Mr. Franklin taught us how to write creatively by having us use the weekly spelling words to create stories or poems. I had finally found my niche. I was a natural at writing, because it helped me to give voice to the emotions I was otherwise burying. Many of my early stories would have made Stephen King proud, as they dealt with the dark side and nightmares come to life; however, Mother did not see the tales that I spun as innocent at all. After Child Protective Services was called when I was in the second grade, she had become paranoid that I would reveal the truth of what went on at the house, so she became ruthless about criticizing everything I wrote, to discredit me. She was convinced that I was telling the world what a bad parent she was and that everyone would know who and what she was, so she had to punish me for it.

In the fifth grade Mother outright forbade me to make or have friends. Having friends would keep me from being 100 percent focused on her 24-7. It would also offer me the chance to be accepted for who I was, loved, and happy, and that was not permitted in her world, because she had decreed that I should be despised, hated, and miserable.

The ugly reality was that Mother was too jealous for someone else to ever be a part of my world. "Thou shalt have no other people in your life" was her first, last, and only commandment, and it worked because for the most part I was either bullied or ignored by the other children. Given the way my peers treated me, there was little chance if any that I would make any friends.

A few children did reach out to me and invite me over to their houses to play. However, those invitations

were often met with Mother's withering sarcasm,
derogatory comments, and on more than one occasion,
physical punishment for breaking her rule against
friends. To Mother, the children who befriended me
were tramps, bad, and evil scum of the earth, who
deserved nothing less than total annihilation. From
the earliest grades, if a potential friend was a boy, she
would declare that we were engaging in sexual intercourse at school and everywhere else.

*Cassandra: I have to break in here for a moment. Let me tell
you what this bitch did, when she [Rose] was eleven. Mother
and Daddy used her to get money. You read that right.
That's all she was to them—the key to retirement. She was
supposed to help pay for their golden years, starting when
she was just eleven. She was required to write to the Social
Security Administration and request benefits because the
parents were elderly. Such bullshit! Who the fuck forces their
child to write a government agency asking for benefits, and
at eleven, no less? There should be a law against that kind
of thing. Anyway, that was just the beginning. Later, every
cent that poor girl earned was handed over to the bitch for
"safekeeping." You believe that, and I've got some swampland
in the middle of the desert to sell you. The whole idea was
that she was supposed to make money for them as fucking
repayment for being allowed to survive, and when they were
gone, she was to be the adopted brother's [David's] servant.
There was to be no escape. No fucking freedom for her ever.*

CHAPTER 5

A SEED OF REBELLION

In the summer between fifth and sixth grades, rebellion began to stir within me against Mother's totalitarian regime. One incident in particular stands out to me. I wasn't tying my shoelaces fast enough, so she screamed at me and I told her to be quiet, I didn't have to listen to her. In retaliation I mentioned our next-door neighbor, who was a mother of five, and she slapped me hard and told me, "She is not your mother, I am."

Unknown Speaker: Mother is everywhere, condemning, belittling, humiliating, and chanting the same mantra over and over: "I am your mother, not the woman across the driveway."

What began in the first grade with Mother calling me boy crazy became worse by the time I was in sixth grade. Even speaking to a member of the opposite sex meant that I was engaging in sexual intercourse with all the boys in my class. To ensure that no one in school could see that I was becoming a woman, she insisted that I wear a girl's undershirt over my bra. Like a scene out of the movie *Carrie*, when we had to change for gym, all the girls saw that I had to wear it, and they teased me about it. Some even went so far as to pull on my bra straps to see if I was wearing an undershirt under my top. I was so humiliated. I couldn't tell them that Mother was making me do it, that I didn't have a choice. I certainly couldn't tell them that she thought I was a "tramp," and so I again started to retreat into my fantasy world.

The shame that began for me in infancy intensified as I entered my preteen and teen years. I was never allowed to have privacy of any kind, as Mother would come into the bathroom to check on me every time I used the toilet or bathed. If I'd locked the door or even closed it, I would have been beaten. It wasn't so much my setting boundaries that infuriated her, but the fact that I was growing up, and that leaving her far behind as the other foster children had done would soon become an option for me. That was what she feared, that her most prized possession could one day walk out the door and never return. To prevent that from happening, she had to make damn sure that I never grew up and instead remained an emotional infant, totally dependent on her for everything. The adult side had to be destroyed before it was even formed, and with it went any chance of me becoming anything more than a pliable piece of clay.

She took to calling me a baby not because I was incapable of doing things without her assistance, such as dressing myself, combing my hair, or bathing, but rather to show me that her power over me remained absolute. I could do things on my own, and I could think for myself, but I was still a child on the inside. The reality was that, developmentally, I began to believe I was still an infant, as that was the message I received constantly. Like drops of wet cement, Mother's message began to harden into a thick, impenetrable shell.

However, despite what my conscious mind believed, deep within my subconscious, a seed of rebellion was taking root. A small ray of insight started to shine, softly suggesting that I could indeed do and think for myself. Very slowly, I began to see myself as someone capable of making my own decisions. I began to see the world around me as my oyster, and I wanted a piece of the action. A yearning to be "normal" rose to the surface of my consciousness and demanded to be acted upon. My choice to respond to this yearning, a normal part of the teen years, was the biggest threat she had ever faced, and with renewed fury the name-calling began in earnest. I had to stay a baby because she willed it. She had created me, and the created thing could not say no to the creator. I had to remain an infant forever, but by my preteens and early teen years, I was not a baby but a woman, a physical fact she could not deny. So she assaulted my emotions and tried to kill my spirit, but it didn't work, for though my spirit and emotions went into hiding, they did not die.

While I wanted to separate myself from Mother's craziness, I could not envision a different life because I had no frame of reference for one. I did not know there were parents who did not abuse their children. I did not know there were parents who would fight to see their children placed in the right classes and would encourage them academically. The extreme isolation I'd gone through during my childhood, combined with the emotional and psychological abuse during my early teen years, eventually caused me to fear socializing with others. I would begin to think that others thought of me as she did, especially those in positions of authority. If others said nice things, they did not really mean them; the truth would eventually come out. I came to believe that I was the cause of the world's problems.

In spite of everything, I began march to the beat of a different drummer. I heard a rhythm that was different, something that was my own, and I wasn't about to let others take that away from me, especially Mother. As I look back on my teen years, it is very apparent that I was not a bad person; in fact, I was too good. I was not immature, but rather too old for my years. All through junior high, the teachers commented on how maturely I behaved, many saying that I was thirteen going on forty. While most of the girls were always talking about clothes, makeup, or the latest TV shows, I was often in a corner of the cafeteria, quietly reading. Looking back, it seems rather strange that no one stopped to question why I was so mature for my age.

What was taken for social maturity was nothing more than me trying to be as invisible as possible so that I wouldn't get into trouble and be abused at home. No one knew about the abuse—not the teachers, not the other kids. I told no one, not that anyone would have believed me. In fact, to me, it was normal. Normal to be smacked around, to be walked in on while taking a bath, to be verbally insulted about my hair and weight— and this is just what I can remember. It seemed no one knew or cared about what was going on; to them I was just another oddity, trying to stay below the radar.

Academically speaking, junior high school was no different than elementary school. I was once again expected to perform badly. In sixth grade, I was in mostly remedial classes, the low-average/high dumb group, because the school administrators still believed I was slow. I was denied access to the challenging and gifted classes. Some of the teachers seemed to be confused as to why I was in their class because it was apparent to them that I did not belong there. After all, I was earning straight As on tests and report cards. It was at this point that the seeds of perfectionism were sown, and Ms. Perfect was conceived and born, because no matter how well I did and how many As I received, it was never enough.

In seventh grade, however, the teachers acted against Mother's wishes for the first time. I was placed in more advanced classes, which caused Mother to redouble her efforts to keep me down. She went out of her way to try to block me from completing assignments and told me that I had to do things her way, not the way the teacher wanted it done. She still insisted on checking my homework, meaning that she had an excuse to call me stupid, messy, sloppy, and whatever other degrading names she could think of. These criticisms were often accompanied by slaps, pokes, and kicks. She was determined to undo anything good the teachers were trying to do for me. The battle to maintain total control was on. The people who tried to encourage me were all liars; she alone held the absolute truth. She was God.

Below is an excerpt from a letter I wrote to Mother in 1995 severing our relationship. It sums up what being in the eighth grade felt like for me.

By the time I was thirteen, I knew what you were about and made damned sure you would not do any more physical abuse to me again. However, you changed your tactics and started verbally abusing me even more than you did before. I felt dirty and ashamed. I was different from the other kids and I knew it. You blamed me for being different and yet who made me that way? . . . I was responsible for being labeled different by the other kids? I hated going to school, the abuse, the teasing, the torment. You don't know the half of it. You didn't protect me. Hell, no. You joined in with my tormentors, saying that they were smarter and brighter than I was and they had better handwriting than me. What little self-esteem I had was totally destroyed by you, and it was done by design. You wanted me to be less than human, not even a subspecies. You controlled everything. I was your little puppet on a string . . . All of a sudden, I was in competition with you. You

*really thought that I was gunning for your man—
no offense, but I'd rather puke than have anything
to do with him. Much too old and not my type. Just
because you screwed everything that wasn't nailed
down, doesn't mean that I was.*

Mother found endless ways to humiliate me about
my developing body. Since I was not allowed to take a
shower, I was forced to take a bath, and then only once
a week. The rest of the time I was forced to go to school
without washing my hair, which was really oily. Every
time Mother entered the bathroom, I knew what was
coming. It was always the same—how fat I was, how
big my "can" (butt) was, and how bad I smelled. Her
excuse for doing this was always the same: she needed
to "wash my hair." By the age of fourteen, I was certainly old enough to take care of my own basic hygiene,
including washing my own hair; however, Mother did
not see it that way.

*Cassandra: Let me tell you what was going on here on
the inside. Livid does not begin to describe how I and the
other "adults" felt about being treated worse than a dog. She
[Rose] was forced to wear her hair in curlers at night so
that bitch could brush and comb it out in the morning. This
went on until she was thirteen. That's right—thirteen! Long
after she was perfectly capable of combing her own hair.
She was finally given permission to have her "own" long,
shoulder-length hairstyle in seventh grade, but she was not
allowed to keep it clean. It was so oily and greasy that it was
disgusting, and she was forced to wear it pinned back. No
rubber bands allowed.*

It goes without saying that not being able to bathe for a week at a time made me the laughingstock of the school. I was humiliated by other kids, who made fun of my oily hair. At home, Mother daily told me how bad I smelled, not only me personally, but my bodily functions as well. Looking back I often wonder if Mother didn't know how inappropriate it was for her to be in the bathroom with me when I was using the toilet or taking a bath. The shame I felt was absolute, as I thought of myself as a piece of meat or a worthless piece of shit, good only for being flushed away. I couldn't even retreat to my fantasy world, because Mother managed to break into that, too, by making fun of the TV shows I liked, the music I listened to, and the books I read. Mother wanted me to watch what she did, listen to the same radio station, and read the same books as her. I was not a person, I was her mirror. My hatred for Mother began to grow, until it simmered at the edge of my subconscious mind. That hatred would sustain me through the next twenty years and help me survive.

Mentally, eighth grade was the turning point for me. Until then, Mother's mind control was subtle, but in eighth grade the gloves came off. We took tests to help decide which way we were to go in high school. The teachers encouraged me to go into law, because that was where my aptitude scores fell, but Mother would hear none of it. The higher my grades went, the worse the criticism became. I really began to believe that I was fit only for menial servitude for the rest of my life. I did not believe I had anything worthwhile to give. No gifts, no talents. I retreated further and further into my shell of self-preservation.

In my freshman year of high school, Mother continued to tell me that I was stupid and worthless, and also that I probably wouldn't graduate. If I did graduate, it would be a "dumb" diploma, a general diploma versus a Regents Diploma. In New York, Regents are standardized statewide exams given in English, social studies, math, science, and foreign language. To graduate with a Regents Diploma, a student has to pass their courses and the Regents Exam. Those students who pass the exam with a 90 or higher receive a Regents Diploma with Honors. Earning a Regents Diploma meant that the student was then eligible for a Regents Scholarship to go to a State University of New York college.

Even though I was a straight-A student, I felt that I didn't belong in high school because I knew that I would not be able to beat Mother's exceptionally high scores in the New York State Regents Exams in all subjects, including chemistry, physics, trigonometry, and precalculus, which she told me I was required to do in order to amount to anything. Right from the beginning I was at a disadvantage, as I was placed in the two-year algebra program, effectively ensuring that I would not be able to take the precalculus Regents Exam in twelfth grade. There was no way that I would ever graduate with a Regents Diploma with Honors, and she and I both knew it. I doubted whether I would be able to work up to the potential that the teachers said I had. They seemed to be happy with my work, but I wondered if they were wrong and Mother was right.

The humiliation of not being able to shower and of going to school without bathing for a week at a time continued until the middle of my freshman year, when my adopted brother David took me over to his condo under the pretense of helping him clean it. His name was listed as an emergency contact at the school, and he had received a call from the school nurse telling him complaints had been made about my offensive smell. It fell on him to tell me the facts of life, that I had to shower every day and use deodorant. This event ranks as the number one most humiliating and shame-inducing thing that ever happened to me. I just wanted to shrink into the floor and disappear. I could not even begin to absorb what he was saying. I had always felt like the laughingstock of the school, but it was worse than I'd ever imagined. How could Mother force me to go to school like that? More importantly, how was I supposed to shower every day, never mind do all the other stuff he was telling me to do, when Mother forbade me from showering and had the only razor in the house? Fortunately, my brother told Mother that it was not appropriate for her to keep me from taking care of my personal hygiene and that her continuing to do so would warrant another visit from CPS. She reluctantly agreed to let me shower daily, and she stopped forcing her way into the bathroom when I was using the toilet, but that didn't stop her from criticizing and ridiculing me, claiming that I was having sex every day, all day, which was why I needed to shower so often.

Soon after I began showering every day, Mother found another way of making me as unattractive as possible: my clothes. She insisted on picking out my outfits and forced me to wear homemade hand-me-down dresses from a cousin who was eight years older than me. To say I stuck out like a sore thumb would be the understatement of the year. They made me look bigger than I was, which Mother did purposefully, because I was supposed to cover up who I really was.

Cassandra: The bitch picked out her clothes for her until she was thirteen or fourteen, and when she started choosing her outfits for herself, Mother called her a whore. Excuse me, a tramp? What the fuck? I want to know who died and gave that bitch the goddamn right to do that. It was her *body. Oh, wait a minute, I get it now. It wasn't her body—she was bought and paid for by the bitch.*

The hand-me-downs were not the worst. The bitch not only picked out the clothes, she went into the damn dressing rooms. You heard me. Forced her to dress while fucking ogling her and telling her how fat and ugly she was. Mother forced her to wear clothing that was too big and ugly as all hell. This went on almost until she left home, all the way through high school, and, oh, did I tell you that she was forced to "model" her clothes for Daddy? Every last piece, except for lingerie. And even those items Mother picked out for her. Mother measured her for bras and panties. And, oh, the comments about how fat her ass was. And she was only a size 7.

Even though I looked like a reject from Goodwill, Mother was convinced that I had committed serious violations of her rules, mainly through sexual deviancy. She thought I was seducing older men and having sex with my classmates during the school day.

According to her, I was engaging in sexual intercourse with every boy in my school, and male teachers, too. Daily she accused me of being "boy crazy" and chasing after boys. Just talking to a guy was the equivalent of having sex with him.

Despite all of the toxicity at home, when I started high school, I cautiously started to make friends. I could not bring them home or go over to their houses, so I maintained friendships at school. I started to see things that I had not noticed before. I saw the way that others had open, loving relationships with their parents. There was love, encouragement, and support, and they were not afraid to go home after school. There was a trust between them and their families that I did not have. I knew they were not called *liar* and *tramp* every day. I knew that they were not accused of having sex with all the boys at school. I was beginning to see there was a whole other world, and I wanted to be a part of it. I often wondered if the other girls I hung around with in high school ever felt the way I did. They talked so freely about their relationships with their mothers that it was hard to believe I was so different. There was a trust in those relationships, an almost friendshiplike quality and a degree of flexibility in the rules that I did not have. While my peers were getting ready to try their wings and fly, mine had not only been clipped, but almost torn right off. I was never meant to fly. I could only watch as others left their nests to pursue their dreams.

While some good things were happening at school, I still had Mother to contend with at home. She continued to shame me for not divulging everything I was doing at school. And what was I doing, you may ask? Working my ass off, that's what. I was a straight-A student in ninth and tenth grades, a National Honor Society inductee as a sophomore (a rare feat, as usually only juniors and seniors were inducted). I was also an office aide, a library aide, and I participated in band and chorus. These were things that other parents would be proud of, but not Mother. She was always in the shadows accusing me of doing degrading, disgusting things with every guy in school. The shame of it still permeates me today. The nonstop accusations of having sex wore me down and may have been the catalyst for what happened later, when I became involved in a relationship with a classmate after graduation.

I have been a fighter for years. Starting at the age of sixteen, I began dreaming of being independent, having the ability to think on my own, being my own person, taking care of myself, and deciding with whom and where and when to have a relationship. You know, normal stuff. From that point on, in the deepest recesses of my mind, a plan was born. I would be the best student in the class of 1977. I would graduate from Brewster High School and go to college and escape her clutches forever. One side of me believed that I would not amount to anything, but by then the teachers were telling me that I would go places if I continued doing what I was doing. I so wanted to believe them, and yet Mother's voice echoed in my mind like a mantra: "You will never amount to anything, you will never amount to anything. You will be what I tell you."

With the advent of my junior year of high school, I should have been preparing for prom, getting my license, maybe working a part-time job, searching out colleges, and hanging out with friends, but instead I was just trying to survive and stay below the radar by not drawing attention to myself.

Mother did not want me to learn how to drive, because it meant that I could eventually escape from her. However, on one of the few occasions that Daddy ever stood up to her, he insisted that I learn how to drive so there would be someone else to do errands and take over for him, as his health was reaching a point where he did not feel comfortable driving anymore. She relented, but formulated yet another plan: I would get my license and maybe a car, go to a local college, get my degree in communication arts, get a job at a local radio station, live at home, and take care of her. Of course I would become what she wanted me to be. I was too scared to do anything else.

Despite Mother's protestations, as a graduation present, Daddy told me it was time for me to have my own car and to establish credit in my own name. With his help, I took out a three-thousand-dollar loan and purchased a 1977 AMC Gremlin. However, like everything else in my world, there were chains attached. Since Mother controlled everything I earned from babysitting the neighbors' children, I had to literally beg her for five dollars to fill the car with gas each week so I could drive to college and church, the only two places I went with any frequency.

During my senior year of high school, boys were starting to notice me. The stream of poisonous toxins that had been coming out of Mother's mouth toward me about the opposite sex now became a raging flood.

Daily she accused me of being a tramp and a liar, and suggested that I was doing horrible, perverted things. If it was possible to feel any dirtier than I already felt, I did.

The raging flood continued into my senior year of high school. Her worries that I would soon escape her were unfounded, as my bid for freedom was half-hearted at best. I knew that I was just going through the motions of attending college fairs because she had selected a college and major for me the year before. I was forced to apply to Western Connecticut State University in nearby Danbury, Connecticut, and declare my major as communications arts. It was an ironic choice, considering that I was an elective mute, generally speaking only when spoken to and considered one of the quietest students in my school and church. I felt like I was being set up for failure.

My senior year of high school should have been a time of excitement and anticipation, but it wasn't. I was not permitted to attend my senior prom along with the other students. Though I did win several awards and a Sons of the American Revolution scholarship, Mother and Daddy attended the senior awards ceremony reluctantly, and they did not mention my winning the awards and scholarship. There was no acknowledgment of my achievements when I graduated. My awards in English and history were never mentioned, and even worse than that, my diploma was sneered at. Mother threw the fact that it was not a Regents Diploma with Honors in my face as the most humiliating and shameful thing I could have done. While other graduating seniors went home to parties and graduation celebrations, I went home to . . . nothing. I spent the afternoon of my graduation day looking out the kitchen door and thinking that my life had come to an end. I felt trapped with no way out.

CHAPTER 6

REBELLION BLOSSOMS

By the time I was eighteen, I was an idealist, an absolutist, and one more thing: a legal adult. I could have packed up my things, taken the money and bank books that were rightfully mine, and left without a backward glance. The other foster children had escaped the hellhole, but I couldn't. Mother was especially on her guard, seeing that I was the youngest and the last child left at home, and she wouldn't let me escape from her clutches. She used everything in her arsenal—mental, emotional, and spiritual abuse. However, the most lethal weapon she had was my adoptive father, the man I called Daddy.

Until recently, I didn't realize how much I was in bondage to him. It was because of him that I did not leave, and I never allowed myself to think about how angry I was about that until now. I hated how he never stood up to her and how she ran everything. More than once I wanted him to do something out of character and tell her, "Go to hell" or "Shut up, bitch," or something worse. But he never did. I never really hated him, not like some of the other foster children did. Those were the ones who could leave without looking back. I realize now that I didn't feel anything toward him, not love, not hatred, nothing but apathy. It has been said that apathy, not hatred, is the antithesis of love. That is what I felt. He was just there, another pawn in Mother's sick chess game, being moved around at her whim in order to keep me totally under her control. She used him as bait to keep me trapped. Trapped by a sick old man and a psychotically deranged woman who thought I was their personal slave. I was the one who had to drive them to the store, to the doctors, and on top of that, I put up with her complaints that I did not do anything for them. Let me explain what I was doing when I was not helping them. Was I off doing my own thing, selfishly oblivious to their pain, suffering, and great need? No, I was going to school full time, doing what was demanded of me. Sitting in classes I didn't want to be in, reading material that bored me to tears, and spewing back useless information. Later on, I was working and turning over my paycheck so that she could control my finances for me.

By the time I turned eighteen, Daddy was already in failing health, a fact Mother reminded me of constantly. Every time I said or did something she didn't like—which was often—she would say that it was because of me he was in failing health and that if and when he died it would be my fault. She would tell me that if anything happened to him, she would hold me personally responsible because I was such an ungrateful little bastard child. I think she really believed I had the power to control his health. I believe she wanted him to die and was disappointed when he continually pulled through from one illness or another. She would never come right out and say that she wanted him gone, but she felt that the only reason he did not go away and die was that it was his job to protect me. By that I mean I wouldn't do anything to help him die. He kept her from having complete domination over me. He was the only source of strength I had, and she knew it and used it to her advantage. Any affection he bestowed on me or any interest I showed in him could cause her to fly into a rage or launch into an abusive assault. My full attention had to be on her at all times, or else. It seemed she could not wait for the day he passed from this plane of existence.

While she ruled the roost with an iron fist and foot, and an ever-sharpened sickle for a tongue, Daddy rarely if ever said more than two words. He almost never lost his temper and became angry, or showed any other emotions for that matter. In fact, he only confronted her once, when Viola was a young child or early teenager, living under their roof. He told Mother he did not like how she was treating the children. She told him that if he did not like it, he could leave. She would stay and do what she liked with the "ungrateful brats." He had been raised during a time when divorce was not an option, and so he stayed, but there was also another reason. If he left, Mother would be free to harm the children even more.

From my first day as a college freshman, I plotted my escape. I fantasized about the day I would walk out of that hellhole and separate myself from The Farm and Mother. But I could not carry it out. I needed him. He was all I had, and I could not pay him back for his crumbs of affection, the ones she had not confiscated, by walking away and leaving him alone with her. I had to protect him, and so I stayed and took her abuse. Freedom was so close, and yet I was too afraid to take that next step, too afraid of what she might do to him.

I started college in the fall of 1977, and even there, my life was not my own. It was an extension of high school, only on a bigger scale. For the first two semesters, I was enrolled as a communication arts major, and though all my classes were general education courses that everyone had to take no matter their major, I found them to be much more difficult than I was used to. I struggled to understand the material. I felt I hadn't been prepared properly for the transition to college life. Here I was a classic introvert, being forced to act as an extrovert. I was saved from further humiliation at the beginning of my second year of college by my brother David, who told Mother that communications was not a good major to be in, financially speaking. Business administration would be better, according to him. Great. I was forced to change my major from communications to business administration, something Mother had always wanted to study. I was to get a bachelor's in business administration with a concentration in accounting, become a Certified Public

Accountant, and have the career she'd always wanted for herself. Not doing what I was told to do wasn't an option. However, she could not control my grades. While I didn't deliberately attempt to fail, I didn't do well, either. I was at a college I didn't want to be at, enrolled in a major I hated, so instead of the As and Bs I had earned in high school, Cs and Ds became my norm. I was exactly what she said I was—a failure—and I didn't care.

While I disliked college, the ability to drive, even if was only to the campus and back, gave me my first taste of freedom, and it was great. In my daydream, I envisioned telling Mother I was leaving and getting my own place and her helplessly sputtering while I took my things and left her behind. I would have a small studio apartment with plenty of natural light shining in from large windows. The pull-out couch would be tan, and there would room for a bookcase, coffee table, and a small dinette with seating for three. I would have a gray tabby who would welcome me home from work or school with loud purrs and by rubbing up against me. My evenings would be spent either reading or watching TV, and there would be no one there to interrogate me and hurl accusations my way. It would be a safe place, my number would be unlisted, and if she found it and called me, I would have her arrested for harassment.

I took a small step toward that dream when I found a book at the Brewster Public Library entitled *Cutting Loose* by Dr. Howard Halpern, PhD. It dealt with what is now called "toxic parenting" and its effects on adult children. I immediately checked it out but kept it under the front seat of my car, for fear Mother would find it. I read the book whenever I got a chance at college, and for the first time I actually saw in print what was happening in my life. I began to understand that in order for me to move ahead, I had to break free from Mother's controlling grip once and for all. As I read the book, I realized Mother did not have the right to control me. To be independent, I would have to start thinking for myself.

Things came to a head shortly after I finished reading *Cutting Loose.* Encouraged by the book, I decided to undertake one of the exercises it offered. The reader was to write a letter, not meant to be sent, confronting the abusive parent. I wrote the letter, but instead of keeping it to myself, I left it where Mother would find it. The response was immediate and just what you would expect from her: "Ungrateful little bitch . . . after I have given you everything. What do you want from us . . . more money?" (Like money was the answer.) What did I want? What every nineteen-year-old wants: to be free from her and her abuse, and to be accepted for who I was. As a commuter student, I had had my first taste of freedom, and I wanted more. I longed to be independent like my fellow students. This was about my future; I didn't want to be Mother and Daddy's slave.

In between my first and second years of college, I took another step toward establishing my independence by getting my first "real" job. I got a summer job working at Topstone Industries as a Halloween mask maker, earning $1.65 an hour plus a bonus for every blister pack I filled over the quota. It was loud, gritty, and at times suffocating work. The smell of latex and rubber filled the air, and even with the windows open, sometimes there was little relief. But despite all of that, I loved what I did. It was the first time I was doing something that was strictly for me. I felt good about my job, even though it wasn't much, pay wise. However, once again Mother took control of my paycheck, commandeering it just like she had my babysitting money. She rationed it out for school tuition, books, and gas money in a way that made Scrooge look like a spendthrift in comparison. She told me how much to put into my savings account each week and held on to the passbook, just in case I had any ideas of escaping her clutches, like the rest of the children at The Farm had done.

By the end of my second year at college, where I was now majoring in business administration, I didn't understand any of the classes and really wasn't trying all that hard to comprehend what amounted, for me, to hieroglyphics. I formally dropped out, thereby ending Mother's dream of my becoming a rising star in the field of finance. At the ripe old age of twenty, I began cutting the strings that tied me to her and found a job as a quality assurance technician at Danbury Pharmacal, a small pharmaceutical company. I no longer really believed that I was not worthy to live, as she believed, but I was too afraid of her to tell her that to her face. So I kept my thoughts to myself. Instead I became, essentially, two different people. Around the house and in places where she might show up or where someone she knew might "squeal" on me, Mute came out, and I acted like a quiet little church mouse.

The other persona, named Judith, was more adultlike, more outgoing, and actually enjoyed being "me," especially at work, where there was little chance Mother would show up. Judith, Cassandra, and the other adult personalities would often come out to play when I was on the job. I transformed into a capable employee who could handle any responsibility I was given. My immediate supervisors were pleased with my work, and I received excellent assessments at review time.

At quitting time each day, Judith and the others disappeared, and Mute reappeared. I had to return to the shell and once again become the scum of the earth who could do nothing right. Sometimes I did not make the transition from one to the other fast enough, and Mother would catch a glimpse of Judith and explode at me in anger. I would curse myself for letting her see the "real" me, and would vow to do a better job hiding the more confident version of me. My real self eventually went completely underground, in order to not be destroyed.

As the fall semester of 1978 melded into the winter and early spring of 1979, I asserted my independence in a not-so-subtle act of rebellion. In high school, I had casually dated Darren, a boy I'd known since I was a freshman. He was a quiet, introverted kid, and we had seen each other through my first year of college. But it escalated to a more serious relationship by the late fall/winter of 1978 and into 1979, with me seeing him almost every Friday night and Sunday afternoon. Of course, Mother did not approve, but I did not really care. She called me every name in the book, threatened to take away my car and license, and tried to force me to stay home. She and I both knew that she could not legally do that, but she could and did make my life a living hell. If I thought my childhood and adolescence had been bad, those years could not hold a candle to what I went through after I became seriously involved with Darren.

Being with Darren was definitely the lesser of two evils, or so I thought it would be. At first when I was with him, I felt I could be myself, the independent adult, away from Mother's grasp. But as our relationship became more serious, Darren turned increasingly possessive and controlling. Since I had been programmed to be on the receiving end of all kinds of abuse, his behavior felt normal to me. He was no different than what I was familiar with at home. He was verbally abusive at first, and his behavior gradually escalated into forcible touching and attempted rape almost every time we were together. I thought that this was normal for couples in a dating relationship. I had no idea that I had a right to say no and to be respected.

The sexual abuse continued to escalate until Christmas 1978, when his assaults culminated in a rape. Not until many years later did I even speak of the rape, because I felt that no one would believe me. Just like my birth mother before me, I believed I had become what Mother always said I was—a tramp. I buried the pain deep within myself, until it was almost hidden from view. Yet I continued to see Darren because I believed that if I stopped, I would be destined to live out the rest of my life with Mother.

I had not heard of domestic violence, or date rape, but it did not matter. It was what I lived with every day, either at home or when I was with Darren. By the end of 1980, I had hit rock bottom and did not have the strength to even start to dig. On December 28, almost two years to the day after the rape, and in part because of a very different kind of man who had befriended me, I came to the realization that there was more to life than being on the receiving end of abuse. All I knew was that I couldn't go on living two lives anymore. I needed to break off the relationship, after five years, with Darren; I would have to find another way of dealing with Mother. I prayed for help, but didn't really expect an answer, as I truly believed that even God saw me the way Mother did and had long ago deserted me.

Now for the best part—drumroll—after I broke off the relationship with Darren, Mother forced me to help her bathe. Yes, you heard that right. She forced me to wash her while she was in the tub.

Cassandra: I have to break in here because there is a memory from this age that has been burned into my mind for all eternity. That memory, complete with mental images, is of seeing Mother naked in the bathtub. I had to wash her back. The feeling of disgust at seeing her that way is indescribable. The two scars, one from the hysterectomy and the other from God knows what, the lack of pubic hair, the hanging breasts, the cold reptilian skin; it turns my stomach to remember. Just the thought makes my want to vomit (but I won't because I'll have to clean it up). I was forced to see every goddamn inch of her, including places that should never have seen the light of day. Those images shall remain etched in my memory bank forever. Isn't there any way to delete them? Please, somebody? Anyone? Is there a tech nerd out there?

After ending the relationship with Darren, I felt so much shame and guilt for becoming exactly what Mother had always said I was that I stopped caring about defending myself against Mother's abuse. It was as if I wanted to punish myself for having rebelled against her. I let her say and do terrible things, like forcing me to bathe her, because I felt I deserved it. I felt that I didn't have a right to exist or feel because I was a bad, evil person. I had committed the cardinal sin. I had wanted my own life. I had gotten involved with a guy against her rules and had deceived her, and now I had to pay.

CHAPTER 7

THE BEGINNING OF SEPARATION

Arriving at church on January 6, 1980, a little more than a year after the rape, I noticed that we had a newcomer, who was just leaving the eight o'clock service as I was coming in. Dressed in jeans and a blue ski jacket, the brown-eyed, black-haired stranger was looking over at me. Our eyes met briefly, and then he looked away and started talking to his companion. Within a couple of weeks, I knew his name was Roger and we were saying hi to each other as he left the first service and I came in for the second. Over the next few months it became apparent that this was more than a casual "Hi, how are you" as we passed each other on Sundays.

At Easter, our choir did three performances of the musical *Alleluia* by Bill and Gloria Gaither. I was surprised to see Roger sitting in the front row for the Friday night and two Sunday performances. After the second Sunday-morning performance, Roger came up to me with what appeared to be a slightly younger female version of himself. I will never forget what he said: "This is my sister, Betsy." He then rapidly walked away, leaving his sister and me to look at each other and wonder what to make of the whole thing. But the ice had been broken, and it wasn't long before Roger joined the choir, giving him an excuse to talk to me after choir rehearsal. As it turned out, he had a melodic baritone voice and quickly learned how to read music.

In July, Roger asked me on a double date to a New York Mets baseball game with his sister and another friend. Up until then, I had kept our fledgling friendship quiet and had not said anything to Mother or Daddy about Roger. (I did not tell Darren, either, although we were still dating, because in my mind Roger and I were friends, and the relationship wasn't serious.) This friendship was sacred to me, and I didn't want Mother to ruin it with her caustic tongue. But since Roger would have to pick me up at the house, I had to say something. Daddy was thrilled to give his blessing. He wanted me to have my own life and not to be tied to the house. I was twenty-one, and he knew that eventually I would need to move out of the house and get married. Mother, on the other hand, was dead set against it, but since Daddy had told me I could go, there was nothing she could do about it. She was quite enraged that Daddy had backed me and not her, but she could not afford to allow a stranger to The Farm to see her fury. So, on the warm Saturday afternoon, I went on my first real date. I don't remember what the final score was or even who the Mets played that day, but I do remember that I knew Roger was someone worth getting to know more deeply.

Though we were not technically a couple, what was birthed that summer afternoon began to grow and blossom, and I did not know how to handle it. I was still dating Darren but becoming more aware that the way he treated me was not what I wanted in a relationship. Roger treated me as if I were a precious gem. He seemed genuinely interested in me as a person and not just in what I could do for him. He would ask me about my work and how I was liking it, and tell me stories about the jobs he went to and people he met there. His sense of humor was genuine, and when he smiled, which was often, it seemed to light up the room. He didn't force himself on me physically, and I felt comfortable being with him. I looked forward to seeing him each Sunday, even if it was only for a few minutes. Nobody at home ever treated me like that, and Darren certainly did not. I was at a crossroads. On the one hand, I had been with Darren for five years, but it was not a relationship I felt good about. I felt more like an object than a human being. When I was with Roger, I felt I could be myself and that it was okay. I slowly allowed Roger into my life, and by late December 1980, I made the decision to tell Darren I was breaking off our relationship. Roger had showed me what real friendship was, and I knew I wanted that. The contrast between the two men had become obvious to me. Darren was just as abusive as

Mother and did not care about me as a person. To him, I was an object to be possessed and not a human being. In fact, after I ended the relationship, Darren began to stalk me, driving by the house where Roger and I went to Bible study. On one occasion, he even attempted to run us off of the road. His stalking continued until he moved out of the area in 1989. At the time, there was nothing that I could do, because New York did not have antistalking laws.

By January 1981, it was official: Roger and I were a couple. He would call me a few times a week, and we would go to Bible study on Tuesday nights and choir rehearsal on Thursday. It was not unusual for us to get together on Sunday afternoons after church to hang out at his studio apartment or go for a walk. Of course, Mother did everything in her power to keep us apart, trying to find any little thing that she could to discredit Roger, his family, and our relationship. However, for the first time I could remember, Daddy stood his ground and told her to stop. He said that if the pastor of the church told me it was okay to date Roger, then he would give me his blessing, too. I took Daddy's advice and set up an appointment to talk to the pastor. Pastor Richard, who seemed bewildered that there was a problem, gave me the green light of course. It only angered Mother even more, but now there was nothing that she could do about it.

I had the opportunity to meet Roger's mother and stepfather for the first time at a family BBQ that summer. Roger's mom, Rita, and stepfather, Wayne, were not like my parents at all. Rita was a small, vibrant woman who always seemed to be on the move. Wayne was a tall, bearlike man with longish hair that framed a wide face, complete with a scruffy beard. He exuded a warmth I had never experienced before, giving me a bear hug when we first met, and he genuinely seemed interested in me. Roger's half brother, Wayne Jr., and half sister, Nina, both teenagers, were also there, along with the family cat, a giant Maine coon by the name of Cola. It was a beautiful afternoon during which food, family, and love were the highlights of the day.

As we sat outside in Rita and Wayne's massive backyard surrounded by the large shade trees, talk soon turned to the annual summer trip to the family A-frame in Maine, on the island of Vinalhaven. Wayne's family had owned property on the island for over forty years, and Wayne had proposed to Rita there. With a twinkle in her eye, Rita asked Roger if he and I would like to visit them there. Roger turned to me and asked if I would like to go, and without a moment's hesitation I said yes, I would love to, and so we quickly arranged to go up in mid-August for a week. I had never been to Maine, and this would be my first vacation away from The Farm since I'd been forced to go to summer camp when I was ten. To my surprise, Mother agreed to let me go. Since Pastor Richard and Daddy had both given their blessing for me to date Roger, Mother had to let go of her dream of never letting me go. Perhaps she secretly hoped I would get pregnant while I was in Maine so she could finally prove that I was the tramp she had always said I was.

I couldn't wait for our trip. We left from The Farm on a Friday night to drive to Rockland, Maine, as

Roger had scheduled us to catch the seven a.m. ferry from Rockland to the island. This was another first for me, as I had never traveled overnight to a destination. Arriving at the dock at three a.m., we tried to get some sleep in his Ford Fiesta. It was like trying to sleep in a toaster, and about as comfortable.

This night spent on the dock was the first of many new adventures for both of us. Roger had been going to Vinalhaven since he was a child, but this was the first time he had brought a significant other with him. As for me, I loved the idea of being away from Mother and all of her abuse. As the ferry—another first for me—left the dock that Saturday morning, I felt as if I was leaving my old life behind. It was indeed the start of a new era for me.

I had ever seen the Atlantic Ocean. Before I could manifest my fear of water, the boat passed by the Rockland Headlight, a beautiful lighthouse that stood guard between the bay and the open waters of the Atlantic. We glided into the early-morning mist that rose off of the water like a filmy curtain. I was immediately swept up as we stood out on the deck of the ferry feeling the spray from the waves caress our faces and hearing the seagulls call to us as they looped and swirled overhead.

The ninety-minute ferry ride took us past small islands with iconic names such as Goose Island, Deer Isle, and others, many uninhabited except for the resident gulls, loons, and other waterbirds. Except for several lobster boats, and our fellow passengers and ferry crew, we saw no other humans for what seemed like miles. This was another world, and I could not imagine a more serene place to be. I could have stayed there for all eternity and never become bored.

My daydream was suddenly interrupted when, from out of the mist, a large island appeared on the horizon. It was Vinalhaven, a breathtaking sight to behold, with its stony shoreline, cliffs, and large evergreens. As the ferry rounded the corner of the island, there came into view the most beautiful sight I had ever seen. Perched atop a rocky outcropping sat the family's A-frame cabin. The cabin consisted of two floors with expansive sliding glass doors leading out onto twin decks that looked over Penobscot Bay. Facing the east, it was a perfect place from which to watch the sun rise over the island as well as the ferry that ran three times a day to and from Rockland. Even though I had never been there before, I knew I had come home.

After arriving at the ferry terminal and disembarking, we were immediately plunged into the sights, sounds, and smells of a Maine fishing village. Lobster boats were moored along the inlet, and Main Street carried the sounds of seagulls and the tide flowing out toward the bay from the mill basin. Residents with heavy Maine accents went about their daily business among the quaint shops that lined the street. It was a throwback to a bygone era.

As Roger and I drove out of town toward the A-frame, I could not help but be swept away by the view. The water was never far from sight, and the tide was just going out as we passed the small inlets that dotted the coastline. The island was not large, just five miles by seven miles, but it was a world away from what I was used to. Large pines dotted the landscape alongside rocky outcroppings that led down to stony beaches. Substantial blocks of granite seemed to be haphazardly thrown everywhere, as if left by a giant child after a day of play. The island was peppered with granite quarries and had supplied the stone used to build some of the famous buildings in New York City and elsewhere.

We drove by small developments with quaint names such as Dog Town and City Point. How they got their names, no one knows for sure, but it was not long before we reached the A-frame. Perched on top of a rock ledge, the only way to get to it was to climb up the rocks to the ramp leading to the entrance. From the moment I stepped on the ramp, I knew this was a special place.

Wayne and Rita welcomed us with open arms. Since Roger's half sister and half brother were also there, Roger and I stayed in what was called the Shack, literally a shack out back with two sets of bunk beds. The A-frame did not have indoor plumbing, except for a line for the sink in the kitchen area, so one had to use the wooden outhouse just to the side of the Shack. I had never seen an outhouse before, so this was another new adventure for me, and it was with some trepidation that I found myself inside it with nothing between me and the spiders, creepy crawlies, and great outdoors.

The week went by quickly. Roger and I spent our days walking down to the large boulders near the shoreline with quaint names like Rabbit and Frog Rocks, both looking like the animals they were named for. Showing me where he had watched the tide come in and out as a child, measuring it with a homemade tide stick, Roger regaled me with stories of the years he'd spent by the water in this idyllic place. We hiked up the rocky outcroppings behind the A-frame to the top of Diving Board Rock, where we could see out to the bay. On another such excursion, we went to the other end of the island and climbed Tip Toe Mountain, another rocky outcropping with a view of Hurricane Island off in the distance.

Vinalhaven was a magical island. I could see why Wayne's family vacationed there. There was something serene about the water, the rocks, the trees, and even the fog that could sock in the island for days at a time. All the chaos and abuse of my home life melted away, and for the first time in my life, I felt at peace with myself and the world around me; I know that Roger felt it also. The day before we left to come home, Roger took me back up to Diving Board Rock, which over-looked his grandmother's cabin and Penobscot Bay. The air was still, foggy, and overcast. As we looked out over the lobster boatmen checking their traps, and the gulls soaring overhead, Roger asked me the question that would change my life forever: "Will you marry me?" I did not hesitate to answer, "Yes, I will." Over the past year I had fallen in love with this gentle soul, and I could see myself being with him for the rest of my life. My prayers had been answered, and my knight in shining armor had come to rescue me from the evil witch.

The next day, Roger and I said good-bye to Wayne, Rita, and Vinalhaven and returned home. Being the old-fashioned type, Roger wasted no time in asking

Daddy for my hand in marriage. Daddy had taken a liking to Roger and not only gave his blessing but also told him, "It will be good for you; it was for me." The first words out of Mother's mouth were "Where's the ring?" She then asked why we didn't elope and get married up in Maine, saving her from having to plan a wedding.

She needn't have worried about me getting an engagement ring, because the very next day, Roger and I went to Service Merchandise and picked one out. It was official—we were engaged to be married. Roger's family was thrilled that he was getting married; he was the first of his siblings to do so. Our church family was also thrilled for us, as we were the only singles in the church at the time and many of the ladies had been trying to get us together. Everyone was so excited that there was going to be a wedding in the near future.

As August turned to September, we still hadn't decided on a date. Mother, though less abusive than she had been, was still trying to do everything in her power to break off the engagement and discredit me, but in a more subversive way than before. She told me that I could not have a traditional wedding, since she had not had one. Instead we were to get married in the pastor's study because that was what she and Daddy had done. But once again her plans for me were foiled, as Pastor Richard offered to marry us on a Sunday, during the church service, and the women of the church offered to organize the reception. One by one, people stepped forward to offer their services, one to take pictures, one to play the organ, and one to do my hair and makeup. Mother was livid that other women at the church accepted me for who I was and did what she could not or would not do: they acted like the mothers of the bride.

Even with all of the preparations well underway, Mother still had weapons in her arsenal. She was bound and determined to re-create her own wedding day, with me in the starring role as her. Mother picked out my dress, an off-white, long-sleeved, high-collared, antique-looking number that was a size too big for me. I didn't even try it on; it was the dress Mother insisted I wear for no other reason than it was on sale for thirty-six dollars at a local department store. Actually, this particular dress was not her first choice, as the original dress she'd picked out for me was a funereal navy-blue gown that went down to my midcalf. The sales clerk assisting us was absolutely horrified to find out that it was intended to be a wedding dress. She refused to sell it to us, and Mother was forced to make another choice. I did not have any say in the selection at all; it was as if I wasn't even there.

Along with my dress, she also picked out the headpiece and the flowers I carried, a trio of red roses. Everything was to be subdued because she was mourning the loss of her most prized possession—me. I began to wonder if eloping wasn't a better option, but I didn't want to disappoint all the people at church who so looked forward to seeing Roger and I wed. I also felt so much shame at how Mother was treating me that I didn't want anyone to know that I was anything but the glowing bride-to-be. I didn't even tell Roger what was going on at that house, for fear that he would want to call the whole thing off, not wanting to have a psychotic woman as his mother-in-law.

As the wedding date approached, once again Mother began to tell me how selfish I was for leaving her all alone in her time of need. Her complaining reached its apex the week before the wedding, when she screamed at me that I had to break off the engagement and cancel my nuptials because I was being selfish in leaving her behind. If I didn't, then Daddy would not come to the service because he was supposedly too ill to attend. If I insisted on going through with abandoning her, then I would have to be married in the pastor's study, where no one would see me. However, there was no way I was going to be manipulated into giving up my own dreams of the future so she could keep a death grip on me. I had seen the promised land, and I was going through to the other side one way or another. If she didn't want to attend the wedding, that was her choice, but no one was going to stop me from getting married and leaving that house once and for all.

Roger and I were married on Sunday, November 29, 1981, in a beautiful midmorning church service. This was the first and only time that Pastor Richard had ever done a wedding during a Sunday-morning worship service. Despite everything Mother had done to ruin the experience for me, it was as if God and the angels had gone above and beyond anything I could have imagined to turn the day into a true miracle. Walking down the aisle toward the man who was to be my husband and seeing the tears of pure love glistening in his eyes, I knew that I had made the right decision. Surrounded by church members, who had become a family to me, and by my new in-laws, I took my vows with strong conviction and deep pride, determined to remain faithful and true to the man standing next to me.

After the wedding, we quickly settled into our new roles as husband and wife. For the first few months, we lived in a condo we rented from David, my adopted brother. It had an open floor plan with a tiny galley kitchen that fit one person at a time. The kitchen was so small I had to go into the dining area to turn around. What the kitchen lacked in size, the rest of the space made up for, with two large bedrooms and two bathrooms. The full-size bathroom came complete with "friends," frogs adorning the wallpaper, and I kept waiting for the night when they would start croaking.

At the age of twenty-two, I was a married woman with all the rights and responsibilities that came along with my role. I had gone from a chaotic, abuse-filled homelife into a relationship that was the complete opposite, but there was so much more to learn. Mother had prevented me from learning how to cook, so I came into the marriage knowing how to boil water, but little else. Roger had lived on his own for four years before we got married and had survived on Wheatena for breakfast, turkey and Swiss on a hard roll for lunch, and peanut butter and jelly sandwiches for dinner. Needless to say, in the early months of our marriage there were interesting attempts at making something edible for dinner each night. After trial and error, and a lot of takeout, I finally started to get the hang of how to cook. Through it all, Roger never complained, or I should say almost never. The first and only time I attempted to make chili, he said it tasted like Raid Insect Killer. How he knew what Raid tasted like, I didn't want to know.

Although I no longer lived with Mother at The Farm, she still had her hooks in me. Even though I worked a full eight-hour shift, I was on orders to call her once a day, every day, and to visit once a week. While the phone calls were short, the weekly visits were another story. Mother complained that there was no one to help her and Daddy get to appointments, and they expected Roger to help them with repairs around the house. Mother, though less outwardly abusive, still managed to make her caustic comments out of Roger's hearing. She still fixated on how selfish I was for leaving her and that she should have never allowed me to go.

By early spring of 1982, Roger and I had been married for just over five months and had settled into a comfortable routine of work and church activities. I found myself slowly relaxing more as the days passed; the memories of the daily torment of living at The Farm were fading into my subconscious. For the first time I felt free . . . free to be myself and let my guard down and engage in childlike play. I was happy and content. Even the weekly trips to visit The Farm were tolerable, as long as Roger was with me. Everything seemed perfect, but heaven had a surprise for me that would change my world forever.

Roger and I had talked about having children right from the beginning of our marriage. He jokingly said that he wanted to wait ten years, to "get used to the idea of being a father," but the Divine had other plans. Six months after we were married, I was waking up in the morning feeling nauseated and light-headed. The thought of food was repulsive to me, and though I still went to work each day, I began to consider the possibility that something was going on. I was no longer naive concerning the facts of life and where babies came from, but it was hard to fathom that I could possibly be pregnant. With all the abuse I had been through growing up, I could not comprehend the idea of being a mother. However, the evidence said otherwise. When my cycle was six weeks late, I made an appointment with my doctor. Back then there was no home pregnancy test, so I did the traditional urine test in her office, went back to work, and waited for the results. A few hours later, the phone rang in the package engineering lab. I picked it up, and the voice on the other end said, "Mrs. Abrams, congratulations, the rabbit died." (For those who are not familiar with this euphemism, it was first coined in 1949, when rabbits were used to determine whether a woman was pregnant. The animal would be injected with a woman's urine, and it was commonly believed that if the rabbit died, the woman was pregnant.) There was my answer.

I was in shock. The unthinkable had happened. I was going to be a mother. A new life was growing inside me. My head spun. Hanging up the phone, I turned to my coworker and exclaimed, "I'm pregnant." My supervisor just happened to be walking in the door at the same time and was the second person to hear the news. They were ecstatic and laughingly told me to call my husband before anyone else found out.

As excited as I was, I was quickly brought back to reality when I realized I would have to tell Mother I was going to have a baby. I had committed the unpardonable sin and was now with child. I guessed what she would say, and I was not disappointed. She not only called me a tramp to my face, she also told Roger that he was naughty. Now it was official: I had had sex and conceived a child, but she couldn't call this little one a "bastard" since the father happened to be my husband.

I blossomed in more ways than one. I loved being pregnant, especially feeling the baby move and kick inside of me. Even Mother seemed surprised by how well I looked, but not everyone was happy about the new prospect. David, whose condo we were renting, told us we had to move out because he did not want a child living there. We began house hunting and quickly found the perfect home on July Fourth weekend: a two-bedroom ranch with a large yard. The selling point for me was not the beautiful Japanese red maple in the side yard or the full basement, but the large, open-air kitchen. After living with the condo's galley kitchen and dim lighting, I knew this was the one. The original owners, an older Italian couple, had built the house as a summer home before moving into it full-time in the early 1970s. Their children were now grown up and had offspring of their own; they wanted the house to echo with the sounds of children's laughter once again, so they agreed to sell it to us. The closing was set for September 30, and we moved into the house on October 1, the same day I left my full-time job. Roger and I were now homeowners.

The week before Christmas that year was grueling. The choir sang the Christmas portion of Handel's *Messiah* during three separate performances. Ironically, I sang one of those performances on my due date, December 18, much to the anxiety of my fellow choir members, but the due date came and went with no sign of labor. Christmas Day started innocently enough, with Roger and me having Christmas dinner with Mother and Daddy at their house and later having dessert with Wayne and Rita. While at my in-laws' home, I felt the first twinges of mild contractions. I glanced at the clock: four fifteen p.m. It was showtime, or so I hoped. Arriving home with the contractions still fifteen minutes apart, I dozed off while Roger started watching *The Brothers Grimm*, the first movie he had ever taped on our new VCR, a housewarming present from his father. At seven p.m. I was startled awake by a strange popping sensation and the feeling of warm liquid flowing down my leg. Running to the bathroom, I called back to Roger, "Call the doctor! I think I broke my water." He replied, not taking his eyes off of the screen, "Go back to sleep, you're dreaming." The sound of amniotic fluid gushing into the toilet and the trail of liquid leading from the bed to the bathroom said otherwise, and he realized it was time. We arrived at the hospital at eight p.m. with my contractions five minutes apart.

Robyn Elizabeth was born at 2:35 a.m. on December 26. Weighing 7 pounds 9 ounces, Robyn was the most beautiful baby I had ever seen, with a full head of black hair. Her bright eyes seemed to take in everything around her as if she was trying to figure out where she was. Seeing my daughter for the first time, I was awestruck and humbled that the Divine had chosen me to be the mother of this beautiful being. A mother . . . I was a mother, a dream I thought would never come true. Like Mom before me, I vowed that nothing and no one would ever hurt her the way that they had me. I felt a surge of love that nothing could ever sever. Just let Mother try to take this baby away from me. I would fight to the death to protect what was mine and Roger's.

At home, the three of us quickly settled into our new routine, and as time went by, it was obvious that Robyn and I had bonded, unlike Mom and I. I loved being a new mother and devoured every book I could find about childhood development and what to expect next. I felt completely fulfilled as a mother to this beautiful gift from heaven. However, one thing kept me from being totally happy: Mother. Even with a new baby, she demanded that I come and visit her once a week and call every day. Since I was no longer working, she expected me to drive her and Daddy when they needed to go to doctors' appointments and other places, which wasn't always easy to do with a baby in tow. She was forever telling me what I was doing wrong, such as not feeding my daughter on a strict schedule, and allowing Robyn to suck her thumb. As time went on, Mother advised me to take away the bottle at nine months, just like she had done to me, and to begin toilet training at twelve months. Fortunately, I knew better than to traumatize my child, and I was strong enough to ignore Mother.

Sixteen months after Robyn's birth, we welcomed our second daughter, Rebecca-lyn, into the world. Rebecca was another bright-eyed, dark-haired beauty just like her sister and her father. Mother continued to call me a tramp, and now, because I had not lost all of the baby weight and would not come over on a daily basis to help her with The Farm, she soon took to calling me fat and lazy. But I had my own house to take care of, and two children under the age of two.

Two and a half years after Rebecca, our third daughter, Deborah Violet, was born. Unlike her sisters, Deborah took after me, with reddish-blond baby hair that eventually went all blond. She stood out so much, with her blond hair and golden eyes, that people would ask me where she had come from. I would laugh and ask them where did they think she came from, seeing that I had blond hair as well. Mother continued her abusive tirades and impossible demands that I spend all my time with her. When Roger was with me, she made sure to tone down her insults, but every now and then, she would let one slip through, and he began to notice something was amiss. I had not told Roger anything about what I had endured growing up for two reasons: 1.) I thought that this type of behavior was normal, and 2.) I felt deep shame that it was continuing to happen.

In July of 1989, I found out I was pregnant with our fourth child; however, this pregnancy was not as easy as the other three. While the first two months were relatively easy, except for the nausea that manifested every evening without fail, as I neared the third month, I knew something was not right. September

19 was unusually hot and humid, and that afternoon I didn't feel well. I had what I thought was lower intestinal cramping, which continued intermittently into the evening. The pain intensified in the early-morning hours of September 20, culminating in me passing a large object, about the size of a beef kidney. I knew immediately what had happened and was devastated to think I had lost the baby I was carrying.

Thinking that there was nothing anyone could do at this point, I waited until seven a.m. before I called the doctor's answering service to tell them what had happened. We went to the doctor's office with heavy hearts, preparing ourselves for the worst. However, on the ride over, I kept feeling a fluttering in my abdomen. I dismissed it as nothing more than my over-wrought imagination wanting to believe that a baby was still inside me.

After examining me, the ob-gyn, a kindly older gentleman, explained that my cervix was still closed and that there was no bleeding, and that there would have been if I'd miscarried. He felt there was a good chance I might still be pregnant, so he ordered a sono-gram to see if there was a live fetus in the womb. My mind reeled. Was he saying that I could still be pregnant? How could that be?

Lying on the table, waiting for the machine to warm up, I braced myself to see the worst—nothing at all—and to learn that I had indeed lost the baby, but once again I felt a slight flutter and then another. Again, I tried to convince myself that I was so dis-traught I was imagining the movement, but then there it was again. Could I possibly still be pregnant? As the technician rolled the sonogram machine over my abdomen, a sight I thought I would never see again came into view: a tiny moving fetus, accompanied by the steady sound of a heartbeat. I had miscarried a severely malformed twin but had miraculously held on to the second one.

From that point on, my pregnancy was considered high-risk. I was instructed to maintain modified bed rest, something that proved to be only slightly impossible with a six, five, and almost three-year-old to care for. Roger did the best he could to step up to the plate. In January, I received the best news possible: I was no longer considered high-risk and would go to term with what we now knew to be our fourth daughter. On April 24, 1990, a week past her due date, Cathryn Michelle made her grand entrance. Cathryn was born with a full head of black hair and her father's dark-brown eyes, which seemed to look right into your soul. She looked so much like Roger that one of the nurses quipped, "Well, at least we know who the father is. The mother could be anybody on this floor." Our family was now complete. With four beautiful daughters and a loving husband, I desired nothing else.

CHAPTER 8

THE SEPARATION WIDENS

When the children started to come along, Mother would ask for pictures of the girls to give Viola. At the time, I did not know that Viola was my birth mother, I only knew her as one of the foster children who had lived at the house before I was born. Mother didn't say why Viola, of all of the foster children, wanted pictures of my daughters, and I didn't ask, but I did think it was rather odd. After Deborah was born, my curiosity finally got the best of me, because of all the foster children who had gone through The Farm, Viola was the only one to ask after me and my daughters. I had been toying with the idea of one day searching for my biological parents but had not given it serious thought until this point. I became curious about a potential connection between Viola and me.

Roger suggested that we contact the hospital where I was born, but I hesitated because I did not want to be disappointed, as normally the hospital records are sealed after an adoption is finalized. He went ahead and reached out to the hospital for me. To my surprise, the records weren't sealed, and they confirmed what I had begun to suspect. On March 17, 1959, six boys and one girl were born. I was the girl, and the mother on the birth certificate was Viola Williams. The connection was finally made. Viola Williams, whom I had known as a foster sibling, was in reality my birth mother. For the next year, I was perfectly happy just to know the name of my birth mother. I had no urge to go in search of her; however, the Divine had other plans for me.

Fast-forward to the summer of 1988. Mother and Daddy were selling their house and moving into a nearby condo, and they had asked Donna, one of the foster children who had stayed in contact with Mother and Daddy, to help with the move. Donna drove up from Texas. In an act of fate, coincidence, or God, while Mother, Donna, and I sat in the kitchen, waiting for Daddy, Roger, and David to take care of some last-minute tasks, Mother suggested to Donna that on her way back to Texas she look up Viola, whom Donna had grown up with on The Farm. Mother had no idea that I knew that Viola was my birth mother, and I did not let on. As I sat at the kitchen table in stunned disbelief, Mother gave Donna a street address in Wilkes-Barre, Pennsylvania, where Viola lived. Was I hearing what I thought I was hearing? I quickly memorized the information and filed it away for future reference. The final piece of the puzzle had been put in place, and now it was my turn to act on the information I had been given.

A short time later, Roger, Robyn, Rebecca, Deborah, and I were set to go on vacation to visit Roger's mother, Rita, up in Maine. However, a last-minute change of plans took us to Dorney Park, an amusement park near Allentown, Pennsylvania, instead. On our way home, as we neared the city of Wilkes-Barre, Roger said to me, "Do you want to look up your mother?" I did not think twice before I said yes. I figured the worst that could happen was that Viola would slam the door in my face, but I had to take the risk.

With the address firmly etched in my memory, we started the search for River Road in Wilkes-Barre. Almost as soon as we entered the city limits, we found ourselves driving around in circles, literally, as the town center is a circle, and on each block on the roundabout there are signs stating that it is illegal to drive past said sign more than three times in an hour. Realizing we were hopelessly lost—and this being in the days before GPS and Google Maps—we decided to stop at the post office to ask for directions. I entered the smallest post office I had ever seen and walked up to the counter, asking, "Can you tell me where River Road is?" The baby-faced clerk on the other side of the counter looked at me with a blank expression before replying, "There is no River Road here." My heart sank. No River Road? Had I heard Mother wrong?

Another clerk, who had overheard my question, came forward. "Ma'am," he said, "there are four River Roads. Which one are you looking for?" This time it was my turn to look dumbfounded. Instead of one River Road, there were four. I had a 25 percent chance of finding the right one. Fortunately, Mother had told Donna that Viola lived in a redbrick apartment house next to the courthouse. "It's the one the courthouse is on," I replied, and the clerk gave me directions to get to the River Road I hoped would lead to Viola.

Back in the car, once again we found ourselves in the maze of downtown Wilkes-Barre, driving on a road leading out of town before coming to an intersection. Neither Roger nor I saw a courthouse or a redbrick apartment building in sight. To our left was a bridge leading to Kingston, the next town over, and to our right was another residential street. Out of the corner of my eye, I saw what I assumed to be an elderly gentleman standing on the corner. He reminded me of a coal miner from the 1800s. While we waited for the red light to change, I cautiously rolled down the window. "Excuse me, but could you tell me where the courthouse is?" Clearing his throat, the old-timer looked up at me with the most beautiful clear green eyes and loving expression on his deeply lined face. His whole countenance seemed to shine with an otherworldly glow. With a small smile, he nodded and pointed up the street. In a husky voice that sounded like it had rarely been used, he said, "It's just past the top of the next hill on the right." At that moment, the light turned green. I turned to thank him, but our helper had vanished from view. Roger and I looked at each other. "Was that an angel?" I asked. "Maybe," was his reply.

Just as the "angel" said, we found the courthouse and, right next to it, the two-story redbrick apartment building where Viola lived. We pulled up in front of the apartment, and I went to the door by myself. This was the moment I had been waiting for since that July day in 1962, when I was formally taken from Mom and adopted by the Salmons. It was now showtime. I hesitated before knocking. I had a choice to make. I could walk away and live with the knowledge of who my mother was in name only, thereby staying safe, because there would be no risk of Mother finding out. Or I could knock on the door and begin the journey of finding out who I really was, risking everything, including severe punishment, if Mother found out.

I knocked on the door anxiously. Patrick Tansey, a man I had not seen for twenty-five years, answered it. Pat had married Viola when I was four, and they had come to The Farm so he could meet me, though of course neither he nor Viola could tell me who they really were. He'd made an impression on me by bringing me a stuffed white cat, which I treasured until the day I married Roger and Mother threw it away.

Of average height, with a slight build, and somewhat resembling a scarecrow with a day's growth of stubble on his gaunt face, Pat stood in the door, his blue eyes behind the thick-lensed glasses as wide as saucers. I knew he knew who I was and was shocked beyond words. "Please come in," Pat said, once he found his voice, "and please bring everyone with you." So far, so good.

Though I was tempted to introduce Pat to the girls as their grandfather, I restrained myself. I didn't want them to be confused if Viola decided she didn't want to have a relationship with me. Where was she? I imagined she might have fled upstairs, refusing to see me, or snuck out the back door. Breaking into my thoughts, Pat said, "Vi went out to get the paper. She'll be back shortly." I could tell he could barely contain his excitement.

We waited in the dimly lit living room, each of us wondering what would happen next, surrounded by stuffed animals, a jungle of plants placed in every window and on every table, and wall-mounted shelves filled with miniature trucks and beer cans. We all jumped when the kitchen door opened. Here was the moment of truth. Would my birth mother—the woman who had carried me for eight months and from whom I had been taken away twice, at three and a half months and then at three years—welcome me with open arms, or reject me once again?

Pat called out, "Vi, come in here. There's someone to see you." The biting response came back: "I don't want to see anyone." My heart sank. Would she refuse to see me and her grandchildren without coming into the room? Undeterred, Pat replied, "I think you should come in here." An audible sigh came from the kitchen. We could hear the slow shuffling of feet as Viola made her way into the living room. When she saw me for the first time in twenty-five years, she stopped dead in her tracks. So many emotions raced across her face in that first minute as she realized who I was: joy, elation, surprise, disbelief, and not a little fear. There I was in the flesh. The answer to her many prayers, and I'd brought her granddaughters, too.

It was apparent from the beginning that my mother was still under the powerful control of The Farm. No doubt remembering what the consequences would be if she ever told me who she was, she stood before me with tears streaming down her deeply lined cheeks. "There's something I have to tell you," she whispered, "but I can't." "It's okay. You don't need to. I know who you are," I replied. Twenty-nine years of forced separation were torn asunder in that moment of reunion between a mother and her child. Nothing and no one else mattered. We were together again.

Pat fell into the role of doting grandfather naturally, asking the girls if they wanted to play in the backyard and offering to show Roger his garden. Mom and I sat down on the worn, comfortable couch. She began by filling me in on the holes in my life that had been left blank by her disappearance all those years earlier. For the first time, I heard about my birth father, how they met, and where and when I was conceived. She also told me about her pregnancy and how she came to live in Pennsylvania, with Bert and John, at the time of my birth. However, the most shocking news of all was the fact that I had not been alone in the womb. I had had a twin, gender unknown, who had not survived. For years, I had dreamed of having an identical twin who was always there for me, helping me out of dangerous situations.

All too soon, it was time to leave the little apartment next to the courthouse, but not before a new-old relationship was forged, this one a bond that could not be severed, even by death. The days, weeks, months, and years that followed were not easy ones. The reunion reality shows on TV depict joyful reunions ending with the promise that everyone will live happily ever after. However, what's marketed as reality is actually a fantasy. The early months of our relationship were more like a honeymoon phase, whereby we cautiously danced around certain issues, such as Mother, while each of us tried to be on our best behavior. The years she and I had each spent with the Family had left their mark on us, physically and mentally. Neither of us really trusted the other. She did not trust anyone to not take advantage of her. I was terrified she would tell Mother I had found her and was in contact with her again.

Emotionally, Mom was a wreck. She suffered from nightmares and severe flashbacks that worsened over time. She really believed she did not deserve anything good in her life, including having me in it, or the blessing of knowing her grandchildren. The years since the adoption and Mom leaving The Farm had not been kind to her. Her health was not good. She was morbidly overweight and a Type 2 diabetic, and her drug of choice was food, which she used to stuff down the guilt and grief she felt after losing me. By the time I was reunited with her, she had had five heart attacks. She would later undergo a quadruple bypass and suffer a minor stroke.

Just over a year after Mom and I were reunited, we both suffered a major loss. On October 8, 1989, the man that we both knew as Daddy slipped the bounds of the earthly plane and was welcomed into paradise. He was eighty-three years old at the time of his passing.

Mom had not seen her foster father since she and Pat had been married. I, however, had seen him just the afternoon before, with Roger and the girls. After a fairly pleasant visit—Mother was always on her best behavior when Roger was around—we took our leave. As we pulled out of the parking space in front of the condo, I caught sight of Daddy watching from the large picture window. He had never done that before, and I thought it strange, as if he was saying good-bye to us for the last time.

The next day was a Sunday. We got home from church services to a message on our answering machine from my brother David: "Pops collapsed at the apartment and has been taken by ambulance to the hospital. I'm there now." Since there were no cell phones back then, all we could do was wait. Just twenty minutes later, the phone rang. "He's gone," David said. In the hospital, Daddy had passed from a stroke brought on by a massive heart attack he'd suffered at the condo after we'd left. The one person who had been a rock (though unsteady) standing between me and total annihilation at Mother's hands was gone.

I was in shock, too upset to cry, much less comprehend what Roger told me next: "We're to go over to the condo to tell Mother that he's passed." Why hadn't she gone with him to the hospital when the ambulance came? Why hadn't my brother called her himself? Why did it fall on us to do the dirty work? I was still recovering from the miscarriage I had had just three weeks earlier. With extreme anxiety pulsating through my body, I drove with Roger over to the condo to tell Mother that Daddy was gone.

When we entered the condo, Mother didn't seem surprised to see us. It was as if she was expecting us. She complained bitterly that we hadn't been there when it had happened, and that she had had to call my brother first and wait for him to come and call 9-1-1. She also stated that she wanted help cleaning out all of Daddy's clothes and personal effects, right then and there. She was treating Daddy as if he had never existed. Not once did she shed a tear, nor did she appear sad or upset that he was gone; she almost seemed relieved. Using the excuse that we had to go back to relieve our neighbor who had graciously agreed to watch the girls, we left after an hour.

However, the hardest task was still ahead of me. I had to call Mom to tell her the news. Upon hearing it, Mom kept repeating, "No, no, no, it can't be true," before I heard shuddering sobs coming through the phone line. In between the sobs, Mom said in a choked voice, "She probably killed him." I could almost believe it, but not in the way Mom meant it. Along with all of us children, Daddy had been a victim of horrendous abuse at Mother's hands. Now he was free.

In hindsight, it is easy to see that emotional damage over the years had contributed to the physical damage Mom suffered from. After Daddy's death, Mom progressively got worse. Even Cathryn's birth, the first she shared with me after our reunion, did not bring her relief for any length of time. In the spring of 1993 Mom decided to write her story down so that I would know what she had lived through. Nobody, including Mom herself, was ready for what happened next. As she wrote, putting her life on paper and breathing it into existence, she started to relive the experiences for the first time in fifty-plus years. Nightmares and flashbacks led to panic attacks, during which she thought she was having yet another heart attack. However, even those events paled in comparison when Mom began seeing the ghostly apparition of Mother materializing in her apartment (even though Mother was still alive and living in Connecticut at the time). Fearing that Mom was on the verge of a psychotic break, Pat and I struggled to convince her to speak to a counselor, but to no avail. Mom was too afraid to tell anyone what had happened to her, for fear that Mother would come and kill her. Instead, Mom eventually stopped writing her story, ending it at the point when she found out she was pregnant with me.

In late June 1994, a year after Mom started and stopped writing her story, she called me and said that she and Pat were thinking of coming up to our home in Putnam Lake, New York, not too far from where I had grown up on The Farm. There was something she had to do: confront Mother once and for all. Mom had finally reached a point where she could no longer live with the knowledge that she had been a victim of the horrendous abuse she had suffered throughout her childhood and even into her adult years, nor could she live with the guilt she felt over letting Mother take me away without fighting to get me back. She did not want me to be in the middle anymore, having to choose which mother to be loyal to.

My response was instantaneous. "No, don't do it!" I exclaimed as a cold finger of fear crept down my spine and sent a shock wave through my body. I knew

Mother better than Mom did; I knew what could happen if the truth was ever uncovered. I hated to admit it, but I was under Mother's spell still, even though I was a mother myself and my instincts were to protect my girls from Mother's potential for abuse. I rarely brought them over to see her. I usually went by myself, or with Roger. In spite of my trepidation, I felt that I could not say no because it was something that Mom felt she needed to do, but I knew it would be the beginning of the end for me. When Mother found out that Mom and I had a relationship, there would be hell to pay, and I would be footing the bill, possibly for all eternity.

Mom and Pat planned a trip for Fourth of July weekend, so that we could celebrate Mom's birthday with a picnic and a cake. Everything went smoothly until Mom announced that she wanted to go see Mother that night, alone. She thought it best that Pat not be there when she had it out with Mother. I knew that there would be no talking her out of her decision to go, and with growing anxiety we all piled into the minivan and set off for Mother's apartment, dropping Mom off at the front with the promise to come back in an hour. In the meantime, Roger and I took Pat and the girls to the nearby mall. It was seven p.m.

The time seemed to drag by, until at last the clock read eight o'clock and it was time to go back and rescue Mom. When we pulled into the parking lot, she was waiting for us, looking very relieved to be out of there. She was very quiet in the car on the drive home, which only caused my anxiety to rise. When we got home, Mom still didn't say much but waited until the girls had gone to bed before telling us what had transpired during her visit.

When Mother had opened the door, Mom was not met by the Amazon who had haunted her memories for years and with whom she was ready to do battle. Instead she saw a short, blank-eyed woman Mom would later recall to be "clinically insane." Mom was surprised that Mother recognized her. Mom was even more shocked when Mother said, "How nice of you to come visit me. Won't you come in? Can I get you anything?" Against her better judgment, which was now screaming in her ear, "Get out! Head for the elevator now!" Mom went inside and perched on the edge of a small love seat, preparing to run if the need came.

Glancing over at her now fifty-six-year-old foster daughter, Mother said, "Oh, it's nice to see you. You know that David calls me almost every day, and we have the most wonderful conversations. Let me have your phone number to give him, as he is looking for you. And, oh, before I forget, George called the other day. He's doing well and sends his regards."

Mom could feel her hair starting to stand on end as a chill coursed through her body. She found herself estimating how fast she could get out the door before Mother caught up to her. Thinking, "She's finally lost it," Mom realized Mother was speaking of Mom's brother David (not to be confused with my adopted brother David). David had died in 1955 when Mom was in high school. She had gone to his funeral. If he was calling Mother, it was from the other side. As for George, Mom's oldest brother, whom she had met only a couple of times, he had died in 1980.

Glancing nervously at the clock, Mom sighed. It was only seven thirty, another thirty minutes to go before she could make her escape. Hoping to move the conversation to a safer topic, Mom asked Mother if she still was interested in birds. Mother replied, "Oh yes, the sparrows come every morning and perch on the balcony railing. We have wonderful conversations."

This was just too much for Mom. She stood up and walked toward the door. Looking at the woman who had been her tormentor over the years, she said with more bravado than she felt, "Well, it was nice to see you again, but I must be going. Pat will be here shortly." Mom left Mother's apartment and headed quickly to the elevator, almost expecting Mother to come after her. It wasn't until the elevator door closed and the car started to descend to the lobby that Mom breathed a big sigh of relief. She had been in the company of a seriously demented woman, but there was also something else, something she could not put her finger on.

After telling her story, Mom looked at me and, with worry in her voice, said, "Now that Mother knows about us, please promise me that you will not go see her alone ever again. I know she was acting strange and she might have dementia, but I could tell she was also very angry with you. I'm afraid she might try to kill you." Looking at the woman who looked so much like me, I nodded and said, "Yes, I promise I will not go over there alone. If I go, I will go with Roger." Mom also added, "Please don't take the children. They do not need to be in the middle. Please protect them." Again I promised that I would. With that, Mom bade both Roger and me a good night and went off to the

back bedroom to get some sleep, as they were returning home in the morning. She left me with much to
think about.

Over the following week, I found one excuse or
another to avoid going to see Mother. However, a
week after Mom's visit, I could no longer keep making excuses, and so, reluctantly, I went with Roger and
the girls to the apartment. To say that Mother was in
a mood would be an understatement. She was barely
civil to Roger and the girls and said nothing to me,
but her silence spoke volumes. She realized that the
truth had been told and the jig was up. I was no longer an object but a person in my own right, and she
wanted nothing more than to destroy me, like she had
wanted to thirty-six years earlier, but she couldn't say
or do anything with the girls and Roger there, and that
infuriated her all the more. The sense of darkness was
palpable that day. I knew for a fact that I was in the
presence of evil, and I realized Mom was right: I could
never be around her again, alone or otherwise.

In an instant, that decision was solidified. I heard
Cathryn, only five years old, asking, "Grandma, may
I have a drink of water?" The voice that replied was
bitter, spiteful, and full of rage: "No!" There were other
words spoken, which I do not remember, because at
that very instant something inside me snapped, and a
power I had never known before rose up within me.
I called to the girls to gather their belongings and
told Roger that we had to leave. Though Mother was
busy trying to hide the fact that she had just verbally
abused *my* child, the damage had been done, and she
knew that I knew it would be the last time. I remember

thinking as I walked toward the apartment door: "Abuse me all you want—I can handle it, I'm an adult. Do that to my child? Hell no. I will fight to the death to protect my daughters. I will do what was not done for me and make damn sure that no one abuses my children—ever."

As we descended in the elevator, I looked at Roger, the father of my beautiful daughters, who had just experienced a small taste of what I had lived through, and said to him, "This is the last time I will ever see Mother again." He slipped an arm around my trembling shoulders and said, "I will support you all the way. Tell me what you need." Fighting back the tears that threatened to roll down my face, and not wanting to cry in front of the girls, I could only nod my appreciation.

After that Saturday visit, I did not call Mother again. Saturday turned into Sunday, which turned into Monday and Tuesday and Wednesday. I jumped every time the phone rang and let the machine answer the calls, afraid that if I picked up, it would be Mother on the other end, spewing her venomous rage, threatening me with taking away my children and worse, but no call every came. As time went by, an idea began to percolate up from deep in my subconscious. I decided to do an exercise from *Cutting Loose*, to write another letter, similar to the one I had written at the age of nineteen.

On Thursday after that last visit, I began to write the letter, thinking that it would be a page or two long at most. Seven single-spaced typewritten pages later, the letter was finished. In it were the memories of intense shame, the name-calling, the physical and emotional abuse, the isolation. Everything was there in black and white. I printed out a copy, not intending to send it, just to have it to read over again. But then, out of the depths of my subconscious, a voice spoke up: "Who are you? Are you a Williams or Salmon? Are you going to be an abused, tortured shell of a human, or a strong, powerful fighter? What lesson are you leaving for your children?" I decided to send the letter to Mother. Her reign of terror and domination was over, and early on Saturday, July 17, 1995, one week after Mom's visit to Mother, I mailed the letter. I was finally free from the witch's clutches forever and could now begin the journey toward healing.

I never heard from Mother again. In January of 1996, I legally changed my name back to my birth name of Rose Marie and now identify myself as a Williams, not a Salmon. I have indeed found my identity and my rightful family. Mother passed away in 2004 at the age of ninety-seven. It was not surprising that she died without fanfare. No one came to the burial because there wasn't one. I would not even have known about her death if not for a cryptic postcard from my brother David, stating that she'd died and been buried with Daddy. When I called my brother to get more details, I was met with a recording saying that the number had been disconnected and there was no forwarding information. I was finally free after forty-five years of physical, mental, and emotional abuse at her hands, and yet in many ways I wasn't. In my mind she was still alive and well, plotting revenge because I had escaped her clutches. It would be another six years before I would finally be free on all levels.

CHAPTER 9

THE LONG JOURNEY TO HEALING

My path to self-reliance did not begin when I severed my relationship with Mother, but actually before I even had children, in what I called my College Part 2 adventure. My mother-in-law, Rita, graduated with her bachelor's degree from SUNY Empire College in the summer of 1982. I had been kicking around the idea of finishing my degree, but it wasn't until my mother-in-law did it that I was inspired enough to bite the bullet. I re-enrolled at Western Connecticut State University in their associated science degree program and started classes that September, six months pregnant with Robyn, our first child. The first class I took was music appreciation. I loved it, and I wasn't the only one: I would feel Robyn kick and move almost in time to the music while the professor played various compositions, and when the professor started his lecture, she would quiet down and seemingly go to sleep, along with the rest of the class. The professor, a gifted violinist in his own right, was not very observant, as he did not seem to notice the very pregnant lady sitting in the front row. He finally did notice when I handed in the midterm exam just before Thanksgiving, when I was eight months pregnant. To say he was in shock would be an understatement. From that point on, he kept an eye on me. The exam was scheduled for three days before my due date, and I was excused from it due to a classic case of false labor. I took my final exam two days after the class ended and received an A for the course.

When I received the first A in my college career, I was hooked. Just four weeks after Robyn was born, I enrolled in my second class, American literature. Once again, I was thrilled to be in a classroom, taking courses that I wanted to take. The sixteen weeks went by rapidly, and I received another A. Over the course of the next three years, and through the arrival of another daughter, I amassed enough credits to graduate with an associate degree and raised my GPA from my previous 2.9 to a more respectable 3.5. I had accomplished something I never thought I could: I had a college degree, a feat my husband and I were both proud of. But not all shared our happiness. Mother was less than enthusiastic about my accomplishment. She was so angry I had escaped her clutches physically and earned a two-year degree without her influence and control that she refused to attend my college graduation.

Six years after I received my AAS, in 1993, I enrolled at Western Connecticut for a third time, this time declaring my major in justice and law administration (JLA). I had resurrected my dream from eighth grade of working in the field of law and could actually see myself maybe going on to law school. However, by 1997, with only five classes remaining before I earned my bachelor's, once again I was faced with the dreaded business courses, and I had to make a decision. Should I take the courses I knew I didn't understand, while hating every minute, and earn the degree? Or should I walk away? For the second time in my college career, I moved my dream of earning a bachelor's to the back burner, this time only fifteen credits shy of a degree.

My unfinished JLA education was not all for naught, though. In the fall of 1998, I found a position as a legal receptionist for a three-person law firm. I was soon immersed in the field I had always wanted to be in. For two and half years, I answered the phones, prepared files for new real estate clients, and prepared the attorneys for closings. I also filed all kinds of correspondence. I realized that, while I enjoyed the field of law, I did not want to pursue a career as a lawyer. In 2000, the firm closed down, so I returned to being a stay-at-home mother and wife.

In March 2003 Roger came home from work with a brochure for SUNY Empire, the same school his mother had graduated from in 1982. The school was offering a free orientation. I could hear the rumblings in my subconscious of my long-ago dream to earn my degree, and here was an opportunity presenting itself. I decided to go and see what it was all about.

SUNY Empire is a state school geared toward working adults going back to finish their degrees or adults entering college for the first time. Empire offered one-on-one mentoring, small group sessions, independent study, and online courses. This was a dream come true for me, so I enrolled at Empire with a declared major in psychology; I was in search of answers as to why Mother had treated me the way she did. My mentor for this journey was Dr. Barbara Marantz, PhD. A retired psychologist who was now an adjunct professor, Barbara reminded of a kindly Jewish grandmother, a far cry from what I thought psychology professors would be like.

Barbara and I hit it off almost immediately as we worked to develop the course of study that would ultimately lead to my BA. Barbara asked me why I wanted to major in psychology. For the first time in my adult life, outside of therapy, I told someone the whole story. Barbara then challenged me to provide a firsthand account my experience as a victim of sadistic ritual abuse. No one had ever challenged me like that before. This was not about reciting information in order to please a professor; instead I was wrestling with raw emotions as they came to the surface.

What started out as a writing assignment soon became a nearly forty-page autobiography of my life. Barbara was so impressed with it that she asked me for permission to send it to the head of the English department, because it qualified as a final project for the autobiographical writing course. I received an A in autobiographical writing and earned the four credits that went along with it. I had finally stepped out of

Mother's shadow. I could do high-level work and was being validated for it.

Over the next three years, I shined in all of my classes: developmental psychology, abnormal psychology, physiological psychology, and introduction to statistics and statistical research. I continued to move out and away from the demons of the past. I was truly doing this for me. Mother was no longer in the picture, and in 2006 I did it. I earned my BA in psychology, and it was not with a little pride that I walked across the stage to receive my diploma. I had my revenge—I had done what Mother had said I would never do. I got my college degree at the age of forty-seven. It took twenty-nine years, but I had done it.

– – –

The second phase of my newfound self-reliance began before I severed my relationship with Mother. Despite all my grown-up accomplishments—holding down two full-time jobs before I was married, getting married and raising our daughters, and getting a college degree—I did not see myself as a mature, well-functioning adult. Instead I saw myself through the eyes of the mask Mother had forced me into as an adolescent: fat, lazy, and someone who would never amount to anything. It did not help that every time I saw her, she inevitably repeated the same litany, reinforcing what I already believed. However, shortly after my thirtieth birthday—the first birthday I shared with Mom since I was born—cracks began to appear in the prison cell in which I had been locked. Unlike Mother, every time Mom and I spoke on the phone or saw each other in person, she would tell me how proud she was of me. She reminded me of how much of a fighter I was and not to let the "witch with a *b*" (her name for Mother) get to me.

Slowly but surely, her words, like a gentle rain, began to fall on the parched ground of my desert-like world. Questions began to rise from deep within my subconscious, questions that demanded answers: Why am I doing this? Why do I keep trying to please Mother when I know that she can't be pleased? Am I really as bad as she says I am? The answers began to come forth, first as vague thoughts that breezed through my conscious mind, though I could not hang on to them for very long. The questions persisted. Was I really as bad as Mother said? Was I nothing more than a liar who deserved abuse? I had no idea who I really was, outside of the labels and expectations that were put on me. I didn't have a sense of self, but rather a sense of being someone's possession: his wife, their mother, her daughter.

By the fall of 1989, what had started as a spring zephyr of thoughts had turned into a storm, and I realized that I could not do this alone anymore. Within a two-week span of time, I had had a miscarriage and Daddy had died, leaving me battered and bruised, unable to negotiate the raw emotions that now refused to be buried. I had never suffered a major loss that I consciously remembered before, and I found myself teetering on the edge of what I thought to be a breakdown. Searching the Yellow Pages for help, I came across the name of Dr. Martin, a Christian psychologist, and gave her a call. I was not sure what to expect, but I was not prepared for what I saw when I met Dr. Martin for the first time. Though professional in appearance, with stylishly cut blond hair that was just starting to gray, and green eyes behind wire-rimmed glasses, when she smiled, the smile did not quite reach her eyes. Dr. Martin exuded a stern no-nonsense approach and began the first session by asking why I was there to see her. My goal was simple: I wanted to find myself, the true essence of who I was. I wanted to find that part of me that had been lost since early infancy. However, that search had been made more difficult by my recent losses, so what started in the weekly sessions as a search for self-identity and self-esteem gave way to how to deal with the five stages of grief I was now experiencing: denial, bargaining, anger, depression, and acceptance. I had no idea how to address my feelings and looked to Dr. Martin for guidance. I soon learned that the last stage of grief, acceptance, was the only one Dr. Martin thought it was okay for me to experience. I had to accept that God's will had been done and repent of the other four stages because they were sins. So, with those guidelines in front of me, and always wanting to please whatever authority figure was in my life at the time, I immediately buried the denial, bargaining, anger, and depression and went through the motions of accepting Daddy's passing as God's will for my life. This was a defense mechanism I had used with relative success growing up, but now it was not working. I could not go on pretending that I had made peace with the problem.

The weeks turned into months as I continued the weekly sessions. I could no longer hide my inability to see myself the way God saw me. I found myself talking more and more of the memories of the physical and emotional abuse at Mother's hands. It wasn't long before I noticed that Dr. Martin was becoming more uncomfortable and increasingly distant as the sessions took a turn toward the dark side. I continued to see Dr. Martin for three and half years. During this time, I read everything I could find about adult children of abusive parents and began to see that my feelings were not sins against God but very real and appropriate given what I had been through. By this time Cathryn was a bright and inquisitive three-year-old. Right from the beginning, I felt differently about Cathryn than I did with my other three daughters. While I had bonded well with Robyn, Rebecca, and Deborah, there seemed to be a special bond between Cathryn and I. As she reached the developmental milestones—her first smile, her first vocalizations, her first words— questions started to bubble up from my subconscious, questions that begged to be asked, but I was too afraid to utter them for fear of the answers I might hear.

By the time Cathryn turned three, the same age I was when I was formally taken from Mom, I could no longer ignore the question that had been burning in my mind since her birth. A lightbulb had been switched on, and I saw myself for the first time through the eyes my three-year-old self, sitting on a bench outside of the courtroom on that fateful day. There was no more denying I had been horribly abused. No one had planted those thoughts; the witch of my childhood nightmares was real. I had been abandoned and left alone. The realization of the truth as seen through a three-year-old's eyes brought to the surface a torrent of raw emotions, rage being the primary one. I stopped trying to put into words what was coursing through me and instead gave a voice to the pain I had been holding from the beginning.

The more I uncovered the depths of the trauma I'd suffered, the more uncomfortable Dr. Martin became. No longer willing to blindly accept that my anger and depression were sins, I wanted to feel these emotions to the depths of my being. I was angry—no, enraged—that Mother had done what she had done and no one had stopped her. This could not have been God's will for me, a helpless child. These feelings were compounded by the realization that was starting to dawn on me that I may have been abused sexually as well as mentally, emotionally, and physically. This newest revelation did not sit well with me. I could accept the other three, because I had tangible memories of them. I could point to specific instances and say yes, it did happen, but to say that sexual abuse happened? I couldn't bring myself to go down that path, even though deep inside I knew it to be true. From the time I was eight years old, I had had the same recurring dreams of being chased by faceless people intent on sexually abusing me. When I could no longer deny the atrocities that had happened to me, I made the decision to tell Dr. Martin about them. I knew that my uncovering the other traumas made her uncomfortable, but when I revealed the possibility of sexual abuse, she told me that I would need to find another therapist, as this was not her area of expertise.

Though upset, I was not devastated. I had come a long way in my healing. I had moved out of the stage of denial and was now strong enough to acknowledge that I had been victim of severe childhood abuse. I continued to journal, finding a safe place to explore my feelings and emotions as they continued to come to the surface. I was still unaware that my personality had fractured in early childhood, so as I wrote, Cassandra, Norman, and the inner children started to come through on the written pages, telling their stories. Once again, there were hints that something darker had happened, something that demanded to be acknowledged and addressed. So, almost a year after leaving Dr. Martin, I found myself scanning the Yellow Pages once again, and then I spotted it. There in the middle of the page was a small ad, a counselor whose sole focus was early childhood trauma. It was an answer to my prayer. The very next day I called the number and set up an appointment to see Anne, and with that call I started the second leg of my journey toward healing.

From the first time I met Anne, she immediately put me at ease. She was a tall, slender, classically elegant woman, with a gentle, almost maternal aura about her. I was taken with the soft shape of her unlined face and green eyes that sparkled when she smiled, which was often. She exuded an air of acceptance and calmness that put me immediately at ease. Right from the first session, she told me that there was nothing off-limits. No topic was considered so bad that it could not be discussed. Even though I had thought I had gotten to the bottom of my early years of abuse with Dr. Martin, I found myself going through them again with Anne. This time, as I recounted what had happened to me and how I felt about it from an adult perspective, I was met with empathy and compassion. This was a far cry from the barely concealed disapproval I had received from Dr. Martin. Someone finally understood me; I didn't know what to think. Here it was, what I had been craving all my life: acceptance. There was no suggestion that the emotions I felt—the rage, the pain, the depression—were sins to be repented of, but rather Anne noted how normal they were.

As time went on, like layers of an onion, I delved deeper and deeper into the darkness of my early years, revealing an unspeakable pain that threatened to overwhelm me. Through it all, Anne stayed steady with me, a rock of encouragement and support. As I plumbed those depths, I once again came face-to-face with the possibility that I had been sexually abused. The evidence was becoming clearer, the first memories coming to the surface. After my experience with Dr. Martin, I was very hesitant to reveal this part of my life to Anne, for fear that she would reject me as well. Toward the end of one particularly grueling session, dancing around the issue of sexual abuse, I blurted out without thinking, "Is there a possibility that it could have happened?" I glanced at her, afraid to see what she might be thinking and afraid to hear what she might have to say. She looked at me with compassion and said words I will never forget: "Yes, it is possible." Though it would be another year before I was capable of beginning the work to heal from the sexual abuse by Mother and others, Anne was not afraid of facing my memories with me, and she encouraged me to take my first tentative steps toward healing and wholeness.

I worked with Anne for a little over two years before I left her, feeling that I had come as far as I could at the time. During the time I worked with Anne, I severed my relationship with Mother. However, no matter how many layers I uncovered, how much I journaled, and how much I grieved, wailed, and raged, there seemed to be no relief for any length of time. I needed to take a break from the inner archeology that I was doing, from being surrounded by the darkness of the past that was coming to the surface. All I wanted was to be normal—a normal wife, mother, and human being—so I retreated from the work, hoping that what I had done would be enough to keep me sane for the time being.

My daughters were now teens and young adults. I continued to journal and read everything I could get my hands on about childhood sexual abuse. I was also confronted by memories of being my daughters' age. Just as I had made the vow when they were young children to not do to them what had been done to me, I now renewed that vow as they started dating. Roger and I had done our best to raise them to respect themselves and to exemplify what it meant to be in a healthy relationship with the opposite gender. It was not easy for me to see my daughters beginning their forays into dating relationships, but I could not allow my fears of what might happen to keep them from moving forward with their lives.

By now I knew it was time to confront my past one more time, this time to deal with the rape by Darren when I was nineteen. I tried calling Anne, only to find out that she had retired. Instead, I turned to the Women's Center of Greater Danbury, which offered free counseling for sexual abuse victims. I was paired with Kay, a no-nonsense counselor with short salt-and-pepper hair and a kindly face that reminded me so much of Mom. Kay had the same attitude to boot. I clicked from the beginning with Kay, as I was drawn to her "call a spade a damn shovel" attitude. It was a breath of fresh air to be on the receiving end of her challenges, which forced me to break through the last of my denial about sexual abuse. She challenged me to go beyond just writing about my emotions and to really feel them. When I wrote about being angry, she corrected me: "Call it what it is—rage. Anger is when someone cuts you off in traffic. This was an attack on your person. No one has the right to touch you in that way, ever." She challenged me to think about The Farm not as a family, but as a cult, with Mother as the undisputed leader. I had never thought about The Farm as a cult, but I could see how Kay could think that. A cult is defined as a group that has a religious devotion to a particular object or person, and that is exactly how it was at The Farm. Mother was God, and Daddy and all of us children were to be her devoted followers.

However, the single most important thing that happened during my time at the center was my participation in the childhood sexual abuse group. Each week I came together with other women who had suffered the same things I had as a child. Suddenly, I realized I was not alone. I was not making it up. These were not false memories, but rather very real ones. I was finally accepted for who I was—a survivor.

After the twenty-week session with the support group ended, I continued to work with Kay. I wanted to feel the emotions I'd journaled and spoken about, but I could not. I felt nothing, as if I had been given a shot of long-acting novocaine. In desperation, I threw out my frustration to God, begging for something that could help me. The answer came in early 2007 when, on a trip to a local library, I came across a book that changed my life forever. The title, which I can no longer remember, resonated so strongly with me at the time that I took it out and read it from cover to cover that same day. I found the answer to what was wrong, why I felt like I didn't belong, even after all these years, why I could not seem to access emotions and feelings that others could.

The book was an autobiographical account by someone who'd been raised in a Satanic cultlike family and had experienced almost the same things I had. I felt that I was reading my story, almost word for word. How did this person survive what they'd gone through to write about it? I knew, or I thought I knew, how I had survived, but I was not prepared for what came next. The author revealed that they had survived by developing multiples. Their personality had split into multiple parts, each holding a portion of the trauma inflicted on them. Each separate aspect of their personality had developed into separate entities. As I read the words over and over again, a lightbulb went off in my mind. The words resonated strongly throughout my spirit. Here it was!

I could not wait for the next session with Kay to tell her of my discovery. I asked her if she knew anybody who had experience working with multiples, and for the second time in less than a week, the Divine provided a miracle as an answer to my prayer. Kay gave me the name of the professional who would be my savior over the next three years, Charlotte. I made an appointment that same day with her.

I met Charlotte in her office a week later, and once again I knew that I had been led to the right person for this next leg of my journey toward healing and wholeness. She was a motherly figure who displayed strong compassion and empathy. An advanced practice registered nurse (APRN) by profession, she had worked with troubled adolescents for more than two decades before deciding to concentrate on individuals who suffered from the same symptoms I had. She said, "Tell me about yourself and why you're here." I began with my birth and my arrival at The Farm. As soon as I started talking about Mother, Charlotte stopped me and said, "I could not help but notice that when you talked about Mother, your facial expression changed radically four or five times in about thirty seconds." I was shocked. I was totally unaware that anything had happened. By now I was so used to repeating my story that I thought I was telling it the same way I always had, in a semimonotone. It appeared that my inner friends were banging on the door, wanting to have their stories heard. Charlotte confirmed that there was indeed more than met the eye, and yes, I had what was now called Dissociative Identity Disorder. This was how I had survived the horrors of The Farm and why I had such large gaps in my childhood memories. I was not crazy; I was a survivor of horrendous abuse, and this is how my psyche had reacted in order to keep me alive.

From the beginning, Charlotte encouraged to me to continue to journal but to keep track of any "voices" that came out that did not feel like my own, to invite them to speak and to allow them to tell their stories. It was not long before they did so. As my inner friends, as I came to see them, told their stories, thereby coming to life, I became more and more capable of feeling the emotions that had been buried for so many years. I wrote about my memories, and in session after session, the different entities came forth to bravely tell of their experiences. It soon became apparent that Cassandra, the part that held the adult rage over what had happened to the children, was the spokesperson for the group. She let fly in no-holds-barred monologues, often using language that could make a sailor blush. At first, I was embarrassed to have Cassandra out, as I normally did not use that kind of language, and certainly not in a counseling session. Charlotte immediately put my mind at ease, stating, "There are times when there are no other words to describe what has transpired. Don't worry, I'm not offended at all." With her reassurance that this indeed was a safe place for all of my inner companions to come out of hiding, I met the adult personalities, like Norman and Cassandra, and the children, such as Arabella and Mute, who had helped me to survive my infancy, childhood, adolescence, and young adult years. It was through their voices that I was able to finally piece together the fractured parts of the puzzle of my psyche and begin to fully comprehend the extent of what I'd lived through.

The more I journaled and worked with Charlotte, the more their stories came out, and as they revealed the horror of what they had endured, the panic attacks, flashbacks, and nightmares I had suffered from the age of five slowly came to an end. Over time, one by one, I said good-bye to the fragments that had become friends, as they became integrated into a cohesive unit (beginning with the children and later on with some of the other fragments), a complete personality called Rose Marie.

As of this writing, it has been seven years since I last saw Charlotte. Of the forty-plus separate fragments that were originally within my psyche, only three have chosen to remain separate. By mutual consent between me and them, Cassandra; Norman the narrator, who is responsible for telling the story of my early years; and Walter, my writer whose words you are now reading, have chosen to keep their own identities. I now know that they are a part of me and yet separate; we share a symbiotic relationship within the confines of this one physical body. I will always be grateful to Charlotte for those three years we spent together and for helping me to put the pieces of my shattered inner life back together again.

CHAPTER 10

COMING FULL CIRCLE

Ever since I reunited with Mom in 1988, she had been in ill health, and in 1997 she underwent quadruple bypass surgery. Instead of feeling as if she had a new lease on life, Mom sank into a deep depression, and with it went her will to live. She openly talked about wanting to end the pain, the guilt, the shame, and all the baggage she was carrying around with her; only Pat, I, and her grandchildren were keeping her here. She didn't want to hurt us, but her emotional pain was unrelenting. She could not separate herself from Mother, like I had, even after her visit to Mother's two years earlier.

In 1998, she suffered a minor stroke, a complication from the bypass surgery, and her depression worsened. It seemed that the only thing she really looked forward to, besides passing from this plane of existence, was when Roger and I drove the three and a half hours down from where we lived to Wilkes-Barre to see her and Pat, but even that didn't elevate her mood all that much. She was retreating further and further into a world where no one could reach her.

As the years crept by, Mom continued to suffer from bouts of deep depression and suicidal thoughts; however, she tried her best to keep it hidden from Pat and me, but I knew something was not right. I could feel a storm brewing; something was going to strike and strike hard, and it did just after Christmas 1999.

Right before the New Year, I received a call from Pat that Mom had fallen and broken her hip. She had been rushed to the hospital, where the fracture was tended to, and she was doing as well as could be expected. Roger and I immediately drove to Wilkes-Barre to be with Pat and to see Mom. When we got to the hospital, we found Mom engaged in physical therapy, and it looked like she was doing much better than we all expected. She seemed to be doing the exercises with little or no discomfort. However, when the therapist left the room for a moment, Mom turned to Roger and me and said in a whisper, "Don't tell him, but he's working on the wrong leg." We were shocked. Why would Mom do something like that? Something seemed off to me, but I wasn't sure what it was.

Mom stayed at the hospital for another week and was then sent home to continue her rehabilitation there. It was the start of Y2K, the start of the new century. A week into the New Year, once again I received a call. This time it wasn't Pat but a family friend, Nancy,

who was staying with them to help Mom and Pat
out with the daily chores. She told me that Mom had
fallen again, and they were afraid that she might have
refractured her hip, but that wasn't the worst of the
news. It appeared that Mom may have had a psychotic
break: she had turned into a raving lunatic, threatening Nancy's boyfriend and Pat with physical violence,
something she had never done before. She also did not
seem to recognize anyone, not even Pat, her husband
of thirty-five years, and the doctors weren't sure if the
fall had anything to do with it. Nancy told us not to
come down to Wilkes-Barre, as there was nothing
we could do, and I was left to wonder if all the years
of abuse Mom had suffered as a child and having me
taken from her had finally come to a head. The dam
had finally broken, and the years of pent-up rage and
hatred toward Mother had erupted.

Over the course of the next few months, Mom
slowly improved physically. Fortunately, she had not
broken the hip again, just badly bruised it. Emotionally,
however, she was no better than she'd been when she
had broken her hip. The doctors thought she might
be experiencing advanced early-onset Alzheimer's,
but they weren't sure, as Mom was on eleven different medications, and there was a possibility that some
or all of the drugs were interacting with one another
and causing memory loss. The doctors made a plan to
wean Mom off as many of the medications as possible,
with the hope that her memory would start to return.

By the time July came around, Roger and I decided
to bring the girls down to see Mom. It had been seven
months since we had last seen her, and I wanted to

surprise her for her birthday. At this point, Mom was living in a nursing facility and had been weaned off of all but two of the medications when her memory seemed to be returning. She could now recognize Pat and Nancy when they came to visit. Not knowing what to expect, I was prepared for her to not recognize me or the girls, but she did and seemed very happy to see us. It was difficult to see my once feisty mother in such a frail state, knowing that the years of torture and abuse she had suffered had taken their toll. For Mom, there would be no going back to the apartment she shared with Pat and Nancy. The nursing facility was now her home.

After we returned to our home in Putnam Lake, Pat and I kept in contact. I called him every week or so to see how Mom was doing. He visited her every day, and he told me that she had her good days as well as her bad days—when she didn't recognize him at all. Her health was rapidly declining now. Mom had developed congestive heart failure, which was not responding to treatment.

Almost a year after we received the call that Mom had broken her hip, I received another call from Pat to come down as soon as possible. The congestive heart failure was worse, and now Mom's kidneys weren't working properly. With heavy hearts, Roger, the girls, and I drove to see her. When we entered the room with Pat, Mom looked at him and said, "Where have you been? You're late." Then she looked at us, and a broad smile broke across her face. She called us over to her bedside and asked each of her granddaughters to give her a hug. She recognized all of them and seemed genuinely pleased to see them. She even joked with Roger and appeared to be her old self.

When my turn came, Mom became very serious. She looked me straight in the eyes and with tears glistening in her own, so blue like mine, she said, "I won't make it through this one." Mom was a shadow of her original self, down to 124 pounds from the 250 pounds she was when we first reunited. She was extremely weak, and her once blond hair was now pure white. Over the past year she had aged twenty years and had no more fight left to continue the battle.

With tears streaming down my face, I said, "If it is your time to go, go with God." She could go home to the other side with my blessing. Releasing her to the unknown was the most difficult decision I ever had to make. I wasn't ready to let go of Mom, because I still needed her. Thirteen years of being her daughter in more than name only was not enough time, not with the twenty-nine years she had been out of my life because of forces beyond our control. Once again, she would be leaving me, but this time it would be permanently.

Despite everything, Mom made it through Christmas and welcomed in 2001. Shortly after that, on February 6 at four a.m., I had a vivid dream in which I entered the white farmhouse that Mom used to tell me about. Going into the dining room, I saw Mom spooning her favorite food, homemade mashed potatoes, onto the plates of those seated around the table. She came to where I was seated, but she walked by me and continued around to the other side of the table. When I asked her why she hadn't given me any potatoes, she looked at me, smiled, and said, "You're a big girl now, you can do it yourself." In the distance, I heard a phone ring, and I wondered why someone didn't get up to answer it. I woke up from the dream, and the phone was still ringing. It was five a.m. I knew immediately what the dream meant: Mom was gone. Picking up the phone, I heard Nancy's voice saying that Mom had passed from this world into the next at four a.m. In the dream she had come to tell me that I was grown up now and she would be with me as a guide from the other side. She was saying good-bye to me.

On February 10, Roger, the girls, and I drove down to Wilkes-Barre to be with Pat and a small group of their friends to say good-bye to the woman who had given birth to me forty-two years earlier. After the service, we went back to the apartment to support Pat in his grief. As we prepared to leave, Pat handed me the urn containing Mom's ashes and asked me to take her home to Carmel, where she had been born and where her family was buried. She had no one in Pennsylvania but him, and he wanted her to be buried near her birth mother, Jennie, and some of her birth siblings. It took a year to do so, but in the spring of 2002, Mom was reunited with the woman who had given birth to her.

I would love to say that Pat and I kept in touch after Mom's passing, but it would not be the truth. Several months after her death, his phone was disconnected and I lost touch with him. Pat, Mom's companion for thirty-six years and a man I was proud to call my dad, passed on in 2009.

While I thought that losing Daddy in 1989 and Mom in 2001 was difficult, neither passing prepared me for what happened on July 16, 2016. On that bright sunny summer day, my nice, neat, and safe world was shattered when Roger, my knight in shining armor, the answer to my childhood prayers to be rescued, passed from this plane of existence to the next, without warning. My life partner and best friend was gone. Though I was no longer the damsel in distress, it had been a great comfort to know that he was always nearby or just a phone call away if I needed anything. It was Roger who supported me when the nightmares, flashbacks, and panic attacks were at their worst, and he was always there with a kind word, reassuring me, "It will be okay."

In the span of one afternoon, while I was away from the house, Roger was taken by a massive heart attack as he napped on the couch, similar to the one that had taken Daddy. He never knew what hit him. While his passing was peaceful, my debut into this new world of widowhood was anything but. For the first time in thirty-six years, I was totally alone. I had lost the one person I trusted with everything, even the worst of the worst. Unlike my physical birth, during which I uttered not a word, my entrance into this new alien place was marked by tortured cries of "No, no, no!" ringing out to the Universe. I was truly alone for the first time in my life, encased in a thick layer of impenetrable darkness, where it felt like no light could ever reach me again. My normal was no more. Because he passed so suddenly and unexpectedly, there was no time to prepare myself.

One day I was a married middle-aged woman, and the next morning I was a widow, planning a memorial service and facing the daunting task of calling family and friends to tell them he was gone. The response was always the same. In the words of Roger's coworker, supervisor, and friend of over forty years, "Jesus, what the fuck happened?" My answer was always the same: "I don't know." Actually, that is what I wanted to say. Instead I told them what I had been told—it was a heart attack—and I left it at that.

However, the questions that kept rearing their ugly heads, demanding to be answered, were "What do I do now?" and "Where do I go from here?" I tried not to think of the obvious one—"Why?"—though my psyche was screaming it loudly, so loudly that I thought others heard it, too. I was beyond numb. I heard and saw nothing. I felt nothing, either, that is until the tsunami of grief crashed into my physical body, flooding every cell with a deluge of physical and emotional pain I'd never known existed. For the first time in my entire life, I gave in to the gut-wrenching waves, screaming out the unspeakable horror I felt, knowing that this pain came both from the depths of my soul over this loss and from the multitude of losses I had been dealt over the years but had never grieved. I was no longer the capable, self-reliant woman I had evolved into through years of counseling. Instead I was once again that three-year-old child who had been abandoned by her mother. From within my psyche, a three-year-old child could be heard through my sobs, asking the eternal question, "Where's Mommy? I want my mommy!"

While I might have felt alone, the truth is I wasn't. My daughters rallied around me, as did my dear neighbors of thirty-five years, who opened their hearts and homes to me, offering me a shoulder to cry on, an ear so that I could vent, and a warm cup of tea. Both of my neighbors had experienced what I had, the loss of a life partner, and so knew what it felt like in the early days and weeks of widowhood. On Facebook, messages poured in from people I had never met in person, but whom I now considered friends. At my darkest moments, I sensed their prayers and thoughts, and those brought me comfort and the courage to stay in the moment, to breathe and to let the tears come. Over the course of the first week, cards and notes filled the mailbox, each offering support, prayers, and encouragement, and all of it so overwhelming. To think that others did care, that God had heard my anguished cries and sent his earth angels to assist in my time of need, was humbling, and for that I will be eternally grateful.

Right from the beginning, despite the shock and denial I was in, I knew that no matter how much I pleaded with the Universe, it would make no difference. I would have to change how I saw and did everything. I was no longer the silent partner, allowing Roger to take care of the finances, the yard work, and the household repairs; those responsibilities would now fall on me. In fact, I needed to make decisions immediately, before I'd even had a chance to process what had happened. Within an hour of arriving at the hospital, surrounded by my daughters and son-in-law, I was asked about tissue and organ donation, and whether or not he was to be cremated. I wanted to scream, "Stop! Stop asking me these insane questions! He's not dead. He can't be dead. You have the wrong person." I struggled to comprehend what they were saying. "Time is of the essence" and "harvesting of skin, bone, and eyes" sounded like phrases out of a horror movie, not my life. I wanted someone else to make these decisions for me. I was not capable of doing so. Couldn't they see that? However, something deep within my soul began to rise up, flooding my overwrought being with an otherworldly sense of calm. Some may call it shock, but in that brief space of clarity, I was able to make the decisions that needed to be made. I said yes to having his tissues donated, because that was the type of person he was, always giving to others, even in the end. I also said yes to the cremation, remembering that the only time we had ever talked about it was right after his great-uncle Noah had passed away. He had said then that he wanted to be cremated, so even though the thought horrified me at the time, I agreed, signing the forms necessary to begin the process.

As the need for me to make decisions continued, from planning the viewing and memorial service to notifying the financial institutions and utility companies, I remembered the wise advice a financial advisor had given me when I needed to make decisions concerning the estate: "Do one thing a day, and let the rest go. At the end of thirty days, you will have accomplished thirty things. Nothing is an emergency." It was this advice that kept me afloat whenever the tsunami waves hit, and it is advice that I still live by today.

Almost two years have passed since Roger's death. The journey has not been without its struggles, but through it all, I have found within myself the ability to not only survive, but to thrive. I am well on my way to moving past the crossroads of this new life and away from the stagnation that kept me prisoner for too many years. I am no longer willing to be in another person's shadow but need to stand on my own two feet as an independent adult giving back to my daughters and the community at large.

It has been said that the best revenge is a well-lived life, and I believe that I have done that and am continuing to do it with each step I take. From the first moment I knew I was going to be a mother, I made a vow to not treat my children the way I had been treated as a child. I would raise my children in a loving environment in which they would be free to be who and what they were created to be. They would not be afraid to be themselves, to have their own thoughts and feelings, and to be able to express those thoughts and feelings to me, as long as they did this respectfully. It was not always easy to carry out this vow, and I certainly made more than my fair share of mistakes along the way, but in the end I am proud to say that our daughters have grown and matured into beautiful women any parent would be proud of. They were not perfect, and yes, a couple of them did experiment with smoking and alcohol, but their father and I stood by and supported them as they journeyed through the turbulent teen years and emerged as young adults. As I stand on the other side of the parenting spectrum, I am proud to say that I have four daughters I am proud of—four women I am proud to call friends.

ABOUT THE AUTHOR

Rose Marie Abrams holds a BA in psychology. She was married for thirty-five years before her husband passed away, and is the mother of four grown children.

CPSIA information can be obtained
at www.ICGtesting.com
Printed in the USA
LVHW101153140223
739452LV00001B/66